BY VED MEHTA

Face to Face

Walking the Indian Streets

Fly and the Fly-Bottle

The New Theologian

Delinquent Chacha

Portrait of India

John Is Easy to Please

Daddyji

Mahatma Gandhi and His Apostles

The New India

Mamaji

THE
PHOTOGRAPHS
OF CHACHAJI

Chachaji Dressed for Work in Delhi

VED MEHTA

Par Kash

THE PHOTOGRAPHS OF CHACHAJI

The Making of a Documentary Film

Oxford University Press

NEW YORK 1980 OXFORD

Library of Congress Cataloging in Publication Data
Mehta, Ved Parkash.
The photographs of Chachaji.

1. Chachaji, my poor relation.   [Motion picture]
I. Title.
PN1997.C3943M4   791.43'72   80-14645
ISBN 0-19-502792-2

The contents of this book originated in The New Yorker

Printed in the United States of America

I WISH TO EXPRESS MY GRATITUDE TO WILLIAM CRAN, who took the pictures that appear as frontispiece and facing pages 80, 100, 106, 118, 152, 186, 194, 196, 208, and 218; to Ivan Strasburg, who took the pictures that appear facing pages 120, 134, 146, and 164 and the shot from "Chachaji, My Poor Relation" that appears facing page 64; and to Jane Jackson, who took the picture that appears facing page 204. (The identity of the person who took the picture facing page 54 is unknown.) My debt to these photographers is self-evident. But there is another kind of debt, which goes to the foundation of this book: in the course of writing it and preparing it for publication, I leaned on several pillars of strength— Naomi Grob, Doreen Beck, Eleanor Gould Packard, and William Shawn—and the book, by extension, has received its balance from them.

V.M.

July 1980

PHOTOGRAPHS

THE
PHOTOGRAPHS
OF CHACHAJI

September 9, 1977

A STRANGER RINGS ME UP FROM CALIFORNIA IN MY office in New York and says he is David Fanning, from WGBH-TV, Boston, and wants to have lunch with me at the Algonquin Hotel the following Friday. "I'm talking to a lot of people about doing this new documentary series called 'World,'" he says. "I'm the executive producer and would like to get your ideas."

I'm leery of the invitation, and I tell him so. I am a writer whose experience of television is limited to talk-show interviews and panel discussions. I find the title of the series somewhat off-putting; I have a dry-biscuit rather than a plum-pudding temperament, and California phone calls, television, "World" all seem to conjure up the plummiest of plum puddings. Moreover, I had once received a similar call from a television producer from Montreal. He, too, had wanted to talk to me about a television-documentary program over lunch at the Algonquin. I had accepted his invitation. He had eaten his way through three courses; drunk white wine and red wine; helped himself to brandy and cigar; chattered amiably but disconnectedly about travels in Africa, Asia, the Middle East; hastily scrawled something across the back of the bill; and left—mentioning the documentary program, the ostensible reason for our meeting, only *en passant*. I had ended up settling the bill, because the producer had neglected to put his address on it and in searching for him I had nothing more concrete to go on than an intrusive trunk call and a quickly given French name. (He was a French Canadian.)

Fanning is, however, gently persistent. I try to get him to meet me in my office, but he says disarmingly that he has nothing specific in mind and would prefer a social setting. I reluctantly agree, and wonder who will pay the bill this time.

September 16th

F ANNING IS UNLIKE THE FEW TELEVISION PEOPLE I have met previously. He is a soft-spoken man in his thirties, with curly brown hair, a mustache, and a goatee, and has the cozy manner of a family lawyer. He tells me that he is from South Africa. "I am a sort of refugee from the government's apartheid policy." He's white, of course. "I've knocked about in TV Land in London and in Southern California. I'm married to a Californian, but now I'm settled in Boston."

He orders a modest lunch—chopped steak and a glass of wine. "The BBC is invading the American market for good television, and WGBH has been trying to do something about it, but so far we really have only one long-running series in the same league as the BBC stuff—'Nova.' In fact, 'World' will be modelled on 'Nova.' But the focus of 'Nova' is science; the focus of 'World' is to be the whole planet. Like 'Nova,' 'World' will be in the grand tradition of the best American commercial television series—'Omnibus,' 'See

It Now,' 'CBS Reports,' and 'NBC White Paper.' " He hands me a copy of a brochure that was prepared by WGBH to raise money for "World." It states the aims of the series in grandiose terms:

WORLD will present political, social, and economic reporting, analysis, and prediction in the field of world affairs. . . . Over all, however, a subject will be chosen for exploration because it meets certain basic tests:

it is in the terrain of global interdependence

or it explores shared problems or solutions to shared problems

or it touches upon the potential for a world conflict of arms

or it challenges a widespread misperception where perception itself is part of a problem

or it concerns the global problems of human distress, overpopulation, underdevelopment, hunger, poverty

or it explores global environmental limits—pollution, resource exhaustion, etc.

or it shows how the United States is perceived by others, or how the U.S. domestic actions or policies affect other countries

or it helps define the rivalry between the developed world and underdeveloped or emerging nations.

WORLD may only incidentally offer the satisfactions of the travelogue, but the seriousness of its purpose does not mean viewers won't be entertained. The struggle of a single man may hold a story worth telling by any of the criteria enumerated above; even the most complex international issues have a human facet. NOVA has demonstrated that it can enter abstruse areas of science without leaving its viewers behind: WORLD will aim to do no less.

"The series sounds very ambitious," I say.

"So far, we've been able to raise money only for one trial season. It will have thirteen hour-long programs, in alternate weeks, and will get under way early next year. Because of lack of funds, we will have to buy or co-produce ten of the films wherever we can—France, Finland, the Netherlands—and perhaps recut them for our own broadcasts. We do, however, plan to do three original WGBH productions, and we are considering India as the subject of one of them. We would like it to be a sort of metaphor for the whole country. Do you have any suggestions?"

"Not right off the top of my head," I say. "One hour for all of India sounds like a bit of a tall order. It took Louis Malle seven hour-long documentaries to get down some of his impressions of India."

"You must have some ideas," he says.

Though my adult life has been spent in the West, I was born and brought up in India, and have written extensively about the country. In fact, it is constantly on my mind. I tell him that I can think of several "worthy" subjects, and we both laugh.

"Such as what?"

I suggest an essay on the Indian sanitation problem, as a metaphor for the chaos, indiscipline, and ignorance of the Indian poor; a study of village India and city India, to highlight the contrasts between old and new; a "Letter from New Delhi," about the cultural and political life of the capital; a portrait of Prime Minister Morarji Desai and, through him, of the country, or, better, of Mahatma Gandhi and his influence on modern India; a personal travelogue of people and places in India that mean something special to me.

He listens without comment. Then he asks me, "Do you have any writing projects about India on the back burner which could possibly be filmed?"

"I don't think so," I say.

He presses me, and so I say that one day I plan to write about an elderly first cousin of my father's, the proverbial poor relation, but that I don't see how such a subject could suit Fanning's purpose.

"What does he do?"

"He is a clerk and a peon for a chemical-supply store."

"Why is he poor?"

"He's had one misfortune after another. His mother died when he was nine, in a plague epidemic. He didn't like school and didn't do very well. Then he couldn't get a decent job. Then his wife told him that three of their four children were not his. Then she ran away with their lodger."

"How well do you know him?"

"I know him very well," I say. "Ever since I can remember, he's been coming to our house to cadge old razor blades from my father."

November 18th

A YOUNGISH FILM PRODUCER, DAVID KOFF, CALLS on me by appointment in my office. He is wearing bluejeans and a corduroy jacket, and is carrying an attaché case. He says that he is in something of a rush—that he has come from California via Boston and is flying to London that night. I try to find out a bit about him—producers are a novelty to me—but either he can't spare the time or he is naturally not very forthcoming. He does, however, tell me that he's an American who has spent some years in England, and that radical causes are close to his heart—as, indeed, he feels, they must be to the heart of any serious, thinking man. He says that he's exploring with Fanning the possibility of producing one of the three original WGBH "World" productions, and that Fanning suggested he talk to me about the India film, because Fanning would like me to be involved in it.

"What kind of film would you like to make?" I ask.

"I would like to do a hot political story," he says. "Can you go over with me some of the ideas you talked about with Fanning?" He takes out pencil and paper.

I mention the portrait of Desai, but warn him that I know from experience that Desai says little or nothing of substance and is not very generous with his time.

"I could warm up to the idea of an exposé of Morarji Desai," he says. "It could be a funny and controversial film. What about other ideas?"

I mention Mahatma Gandhi, but say I feel sure he will agree that that is too large a subject for a short documentary.

"Gandhi is a little too goody-goody for me," he says.

I mention the lack of sanitation and the spread of disease and poverty, but tell him that a film on such a subject would be visually so repulsive that it could perhaps not be shown on television at all.

"That's an explosive idea," he says. "I could really go for it."

He asks me if he may talk to me further from London, and we make a transatlantic-telephone appointment for twelve-thirty the next day. "Frankly, I don't understand why Fanning wants a writer involved," Koff says as he is leaving. "It's bound to steal the thunder from the producer and set up a situation for conflict. Still, I feel that your advice on a film about India could be a boon."

November 19th

K OFF AND I TALK FOR HALF AN HOUR, GOING OVER more or less the same ground. At one point, I worry aloud about the cost of the transatlantic call, and Koff says to me reassuringly, "It's part of the expense of making a film."

December 12th

K OFF RINGS UP FROM BOSTON TO SAY THAT WGBH
has hired him to do a film about England but
is still going ahead with the India film—with
a different producer. "I feel I have a proprietary interest in the India film," he says. "And
I would like to fly down with the new producer and sit in on the discussions. I wish we were doing the India film in the second season. Then I could
produce it, too."

"Who is the new producer? Do they have one?" I
ask, somewhat nonplussed. No one from WGBH has
discussed with me the exact terms of my participation.

"It's not been completely decided yet, but I think
it will be a Canadian—or, rather, a Tasmanian. His
name is Bill Cran. I must tell you that they may want
you only for consultation. From now on, they will pay
you something for your time. Cran and I want to
come down this Saturday. Is that all right with you?"

I say yes, but without being quite clear just what I
am agreeing to.

December 17th

J UST AFTER ELEVEN IN THE MORNING, NOT KOFF but Fanning arrives at my apartment. He is accompanied by a tall, cherubic-looking man in a brown corduroy suit. The newcomer, who appears to be in his early thirties, has a long jaw, thin lips, and very curly brown hair, so thick and abundant that the curls seem to sit on his head like a helmet. His eyes, a light hazel, dart around the room, from the bookcase to the window to the pictures on the wall, as if he were trying to size up the room for a shot. He introduces himself as Bill Cran. "Bill," he says emphatically.

I assume that we will get down to talking about the India film right away, but Bill seems to be in no hurry. He takes a pipe and a pouch out of his pocket, fills the pipe, lights it, and plunges into stories, some of them funny, about covering the Watergate hearings for the BBC and about location work in Northern Ireland and Cyprus. He talks fast but has a good sense of timing and is able to squeeze the last meaning from a detail. He laughs a lot at his own funny stories, in a nervous but infectious way, and it is hard to resist him. There is something schoolboyish about him—an impression strengthened by a faint lisp. At the same time, he has a no-nonsense, knowledgeable way of speaking, with a slightly hard edge to his voice.

Finally, Fanning says, "I would like you to go to India with Bill, as a writer—we will discuss the terms with your agent—and the two of you can make any film you like, provided you agree on it. Can we review the ideas we discussed over lunch?"

The discussion goes quickly, because it soon turns out that Fanning has really taken to the idea of a film about my poor relation. "Ever since you told me about that poor old man cadging razor blades from your father, I haven't been able to get him out of my head. I told my colleagues in Boston about him, and they were as charmed and haunted by the story as I was. I've had a picture of this old man coming to beg a blade from your father every morning and then tearing through Delhi on a rickety old bicycle delivering medicines to the sick. As he goes on his rounds, we could show different parts of Delhi. There is something poignant in the idea of an old man who needs mercy himself going on rounds of mercy."

"Actually, he doesn't ride a bicycle anymore," I say. "He's too old and frail to maneuver it through Delhi traffic."

"What do you call the old sod?" Bill asks.

"Chachaji—it means 'Respected Uncle.' 'Ji' after any name signifies respect and affection."

Bill wants to make what he calls a crib sheet, so we start drawing up a sort of shopping list of scenes. The three of us talk excitedly about doing a "day-in-the-life-of" film about Chachaji. In my mind, he is becoming the hero of a Victorian novel with such chapter headings as: In Which Chachaji Wakes Up; In Which

Chachaji Cleans His Teeth with a Lot of Hacking; In Which Our Hero Ties His Turban and Goes Out; In Which Chachaji Drops by the House of a Rich Relation for Bed Tea; In Which Chachaji Cadges Razor Blades; In Which Our Hero Waits in a Queue for a Bottle of Milk; In Which Chachaji Fights His Way Through the Bazaars and Arrives at the Apothecary Shop for Which He Is a Messenger.

"That's it, then," Fanning says. "You'll do Chacha, unless he dies or turns out to be uncoöperative or a terribly bad actor—in which case the two of you will simply have to come up with a good idea on the spot."

"I have no idea how Chachaji is these days," I say, sobering a little. "For all I know, he may be sick."

"We'll film him in bed," Bill says. "In any case, we'll improvise. Talking about Chacha and poor people has made me hungry. Let's eat."

We go out to a nearby hotel for lunch, and begin to plan the technical arrangements for shooting the film.

"You and I should go to India a month ahead of the crew," Bill says. "We'll have to get various government permits and clearances, we'll have to choose locations, we'll have to line up shots and look over Chacha and his supporting cast."

I demur. "I think we should all arrive in India together," I say. "We could spend weeks organizing the locations and people, and then when the crew gets there to film, all our arrangements could fall apart. People can get scared or, for mysterious reasons, not be where you expect them to be. Also, if it's to be a true family picture we must have the camera at the ready to take advantage of chance occurrences, spontaneous moments. Let's say that we arrive in the middle of some family gathering. It would be heartbreaking not to be able to film it. And if it was staged it would never be the same."

"You don't understand the power of television," Bill says. "When people see that the camera is turned on, they start behaving like their real selves. All the dead, superficial stuff falls off."

"I don't want people to do things for the camera," I say. "I want the camera to be as nearly an invisible presence as possible."

Fanning gently points out that I am talking like a writer who is naïve about the way television works, and that we have to plan carefully, because we are to make a documentary in color, which is a very expensive business.

"I don't like the idea of having an expensive crew on my back—having them sitting around waiting and doing nothing," Bill says. "An idle crew will get demoralized very quickly, and then you can't get any work out of them. They become slothful, disobedient, disrespectful, like idle soldiers. We could run out of money before we've taken a single picture."

"I take responsibility for keeping the crew busy," I say. "There will be plenty to shoot."

"What about our arriving just a few days ahead of the crew and staking out the ground and limbering up the family?" Bill asks.

I hold to my faith that spontaneity is all-important

to the kind of film I have in mind, and say that, in any case, if for some reason the Chacha film shouldn't work out, we couldn't possibly go to a country as rich in material as India and end up with nothing. As it turns out, I get my way only when I say, "Knowing India, I'm afraid that if we arrived before the crew they might be let in but their equipment might be impounded, or even sent back, because they didn't have some official paper or other. If we were all together, that would be less likely to happen."

So it is agreed that Bill, the crew, and I will go to India together and take our chances with the authorities, the family, and Chachaji.

"What can I tell you?" Bill says, throwing up his hands in feigned exasperation. "We'll simply have to fly by the seat of our pants all the way. Our filming methods are just going to have to be different. We won't do any research on locations before we shoot. We won't have a script, or even a definite idea of the precise story. But at least we will have a writer on the team. Most documentaries are brought in by just a producer, a cameraman, and a sound recordist."

Fanning, changing the subject, mentions "I, Claudius," which is currently playing on "Masterpiece Theatre."

"Although none of the history is really the way things happened, BBC scores again," Bill says. "We have to beat it at its own game. The question is not whether we can make a good film—as you say, how could we miss?—but whether we can make one that will get a prize."

December 22nd

MY AGENT HAS SENT ME THE TELEVISION CONTRACT from WGBH. I am struck by how different it is from a book contract. By signing it, I will commit myself not only to being a writer (familiar ground) but also to being part actor, part commentator, part consultant, part producer (strange territory). Moreover, I've never signed a book contract until the book existed on paper. I must, however, sign the television contract before a single shot has been taken—or, for that matter, before the proposed hero of our drama has given his informed consent to its filming. I cabled my father to find out how Chachaji felt about the project, and got the answer that Chachaji didn't know what a moving picture was and that it was impossible to explain it to him but that he had said, "You are all my government. I will do whatever my beloved second cousin from America orders."

January 19, 1978

I TELEPHONE THE CONSUL GENERAL OF INDIA IN New York, K. Srinivasan, tell him about our project, and ask him about the formalities that are necessary to enable a foreign film team to work in India.

"I'm sorry, but no one can shoot a film in India without clearances from the highest authorities in Delhi," he says. "To get the necessary clearances, you must agree to have attached to your film unit an official escort of the government's choosing who will have veto power over everything that is shot. You must also undertake to pay his board, lodging, and travel expenses for the period of the shooting. You must also agree to show a designated official of the government here in New York a rough cut of the film and agree that you will broadcast nothing that has not been approved by this official."

From years of writing about India, I am all too familiar with the bureaucratic hurdles placed in the path of anyone who plans to work in India for a foreign organization, but I also know that there are often ways around them and that the hurdles sound more forbidding than they really are—at least, than they are for people who are known to the Indian government. I explain to the Consul General that the proposed theme of the film is my family—in particular, a poor cousin of my father's—and that the film is intended for the Public Broadcasting Service. "Do you think you could get us an exemption from the rule of official escort?" I ask.

"Since you are involved in the project, I will try my best," he says. "The government may be persuaded to take the view that you are going on a private visit to your family and making something educational. But we would still have to insist on our right of approval of the rough cut in New York—though I'm sure it would be mostly a formality, since you wouldn't want to embarrass us."

I know from experience that "not embarrass" is a code phrase for not focussing on Indian poverty. India has more poor people today than any other country has had in the history of the world, and Indian officials feel that depictions of these people give the country a "bad image" and discourage the tourist trade. But I also know that, as a rule, Indian officials who work in this country tend to be much less sensitive about such things than their colleagues at home.

"I don't know about embarrassing the government, but I'm sure our film will portray the country in a sympathetic light," I say. "In any case, a government that ousted Mrs. Gandhi and came to power on the cry of civil liberties and freedom of the press would not want to inhibit freedom of expression, would it?"

"No, no," he says. "Please give the details about the film unit and the film goods you want to import to our Public Relations Consul here. They must be forwarded to Delhi for clearances."

I am switched to the Public Relations Consul.

January 24th

B ILL RINGS UP FROM TORONTO AND SAYS, "I AM coming to New York Saturday week. Can we thrash out the plans for the film then? The Missus will be with me. It'll be your and my last-but-one weekend in these parts." We have settled on February 17th as our departure date. "I would like to treat the Missus to a little holiday to make up for the month I'll be away from her. I have booked us into the Algonquin. The 'Missus' business is a jokey way I have of talking about my wife. It really gets her riled up."

February 4th

A T 10:30 A.M., BILL ARRIVES AT MY APARTMENT with his wife, a sturdy, imposing woman. Her hair is a little untidy and she is casually dressed in slacks, a tunic top, and boots. There is something stark and intellectual about her appearance; she gives the impression of a classic bluestocking.

"The Missus was at Oxford, too, like you and me," Bill says, with his infectious laugh. "She read English."

"I only answer to Araminta Wordsworth," she says, a little haughtily but not sharply, as if the name business were a routine between them. "The poet was my great-great-granduncle. Please call me Araminta."

"Imagine having Wordsworth for your Chacha," Bill says, settling in and lighting his pipe. Araminta doesn't laugh, and he goes on, "I may not have a grand pedigree, but, after all, Mrs. Cran, was I not one of six undergraduates chosen out of more than nine hundred applicants by the BBC for its general-trainee program?" Turning to me, he says, "I could have had a lifelong career with the BBC, but I found it was just too comfortable a slot, so I left for Canada and the CBC. No one ever leaves the BBC, and because I did, my stock has been going up with them ever since. They make me a new offer almost every time I see them. One way to get people to want you is to leave them."

"The decision to leave England must have been a difficult one," I say.

"It was," he says. "Araminta, especially, didn't want to leave—she's so English, you know. But if we hadn't left, I would not have had the opportunity to do this film with you."

I start telling Bill about my conversation with the Consul General, and Araminta picks up a book and looks through it.

"God, imagine a government flunky at our elbow all the time telling us what we should and shouldn't do," Bill says. "Perhaps I could take care of him with hooch and victuals." Like many Oxford-educated men, Bill sprinkles his talk with vivid colloquialisms. "He might be so incompetent he wouldn't really know what we were doing. Anyway, our 16-mm. film stock is in color, which can't be developed in India, so they won't be able to check up on what we've shot. But giving editorial control of the rough cut to someone in New York—that's another matter."

I reassure him about the rough cut. "We could agree to a government official's looking it over, take notes on his suggestions, and then, if we don't like them, make a stand on freedom of the press," I say.

"O.K.," Bill says, with a laugh.

Araminta looks up from her book and says, "What about lunch, chaps? I'm starving."

We walk over to a nearby delicatessen.

Araminta is excited about being in a delicatessen in New York—she hasn't spent much time in the city—and orders specialties of the house, including matzo-ball soup. "I'm very jealous of you chaps, tooling around India with all expenses paid," she says. "Why can't you put me on the film team, Bill?"

"You have your job in Toronto with the *Financial Post,*" he replies. "Besides, women on film units always create problems. If I had my way, my film unit would have only men. Women are nice in drawing rooms." He laughs.

After lunch, Bill says, "Araminta, why don't you go shop for those books and boots you wanted while we continue with our work."

He hands her some American money, and she sets off in the direction of Fifth Avenue, calling over her shoulder, "I'll be back around five."

"What films have you done that I may have heard of?" I ask Bill as we head back to my apartment.

"You may not have heard of any of them," he says. Then he tells me that in the last ten years or so he has worked for British, Canadian, and American television, specializing in investigative documentaries and current-affairs programs, and filming in twenty-one countries, on four continents. He has produced—or assisted in the production of—about a hundred short films and some fifteen full-length documentaries, including "The Agony of Cyprus," "Portugal: The Fight for Empire," "Saudi Arabia: Land of Oil and Money," "Cuba: The New Man," and "Who Fights for Rhodesia?" "But there's only one film I'm really proud of, and I think that it's the only one Fanning saw and that he actually chose me because of it," he says. "That's 'The Agony of Cyprus.' It deals with the aftermath of the latest Cyprus war—the refugees, the divided families, the missing sons and husbands. There were just three of us—camera, sound, and me—and we were lucky. We arrived right at the end of the war, and people were so busy grieving for their dead that no one took much notice of us. We happened to latch onto a Greek priest who had just lost his son in the war. We were able to follow him around and get all his grief on film. The film was so excruciating that I could scarcely bear to have a private screening for the critics. I think I even avoided seeing the film when it was shown on the telly."

Bill and I reach my apartment, and he picks up paper and pencil, and asks me, "Are there any formal occasions when your family regularly gets together?"

"Not as such. But, as it happens, my sister Nimi's daughter Rajani will be getting married around the time we arrive."

"How did she meet the man?" Bill asks.

"Nimi and her husband, Mahesh, advertised in the matrimonial columns, like practically everyone else."

Bill, who is writing everything down, gets excited. "What does Mahesh do?"

"He's the managing director of Indian Airlines, the government-owned domestic carrier."

"We could show Mahesh dressed up like a modern executive driving from the airport, with a jumbo jet in the background, and arriving at the newspaper office to place his ad. We could show the presses rolling and the pages coming out and then being hawked all over the bazaars. Then we could zoom in on an innocent-looking fellow stumbling along the road and arriving at Mahesh's big house to offer himself as a candidate. What do the bride and groom do in the tradition of arranged marriages—have tea together, or something? Isn't there a wedding horse? We could make a wonderful little sequence."

I am amused by Bill's leaps of imagination, but I explain that marriages are not arranged in quite the mechanical, predatory way he thinks. Then I ask him if the financing of the film is all in hand.

"WGBH has it well under control or we wouldn't have got the green light," he tells me. "There is a lot of lolly riding on us. The total budget of the film, from soup to nuts, is a hundred and fifty thousand dollars: forty thousand dollars for film stock and for developing, editing, and printing; I don't know exactly how much for developing the idea, for overhead, for promotion, and whatnot; probably ten thousand dollars or so for you and your expenses and your assistant's expenses; and forty thousand dollars for me, as subcontracting producer. I am responsible for all the travel and living expenses of the crew—cameraman, camera assistant, and sound recordist. Of course, I subcontract the actual work as well. WGBH wanted me to subcontract you and your assistant, too, as part of the team, but I thought that that would be bad for our relationship— I felt we should both be working for WGBH. They will be paying your fees and expenses directly. I'm going to look for an English crew, because they're cheaper and better. English camera makes about eight hundred dollars a week, English sound about six hundred dollars a week, and an English camera assistant about four hundred dollars a week." For "cameraman" and "sound recordist," I have come to realize, Bill often uses television jargon—"camera" and "sound." "The subcontracting for four weeks of shooting will cost me, I reckon, about seventy-two hundred dollars all told. Whatever is left over after paying all the crew's living and travelling expenses is gravy for me."

"It would be nice to find a cameraman who is good at hand-held work, so that we could shoot with as little fuss as possible," I say. "He should also be good at working in natural light, since bright lights could be inhibiting."

"That should be no problem," Bill says, puffing at his pipe. "I know who the good cameras are. The documentary world is a very small world. Ivan Strasburg would be excellent. So would Ernest Vincze, but he's not free. Erik Durschmied would also be excellent, but he's not in my price range. There isn't much of a market for documentaries. Everybody knows everybody.

By the way, there's an Indian camera who's surfaced in Toronto and who's been after me for some work. I've heard good things about him, but I haven't seen anything he's done. Perhaps I should check it out."

"Unless he's as good as Subrata Mitra, who has done so much work for Satyajit Ray, I would prefer a foreigner—if possible, one who has never been to India—so that he would see the country with fresh eyes," I say.

"The one I have settled on in my mind is Ivan Strasburg. He's a South African political refugee who lives and works out of England," Bill says. "He is light on his feet and good with hand-held stuff and can work in natural light fine."

February 8th

BILL TELEPHONES ME IN THE MORNING FROM Boston. "God damn this blizzard," he says. "I've been stuck here with the Fannings for four whole days, and I came only for a few hours to say goodbye. The snow is so thick we can scarcely get out of the house. And we're all getting on each other's nerves."

He and I go over the latest arrangements.

"Ivan Strasburg had already started working on Koff's film, but Fanning has sprung him loose for us," Bill says. "Ivan has arranged for his acolyte, Jane Jackson, to be the camera assistant. Eoin McCann will be our sound. By the way, when I told Ivan that you wanted most of the shooting done in natural light, you know what he said? 'Not for nothing am I known as the Prince of Darkness.' " Bill laughs.

I tell him that I've arranged for an assistant—Sally Sandberg, Bennington '77, who has been working with the literary agent Georges Borchardt. I also tell him that, as I expected, the Indian government has given us an exemption from the "escort rule," but that it urgently needs a list of the members of our film team, an itemization of our film stock and equipment, and the details of our arrival plans.

Bill gives me the following information about the equipment and film stock we'll be taking to India: one Eclair (NPR) camera; two batteries, two battery chargers; one 12-120-mm. zoom lens; one 16-44-mm. zoom lens; one wide-angle 10-mm. lens; one Miller tripod (tall and short legs); one Lowel Tota-Light kit (5 heads); two light meters; one Nagra tape recorder; six microphones; cables, charger, and other tape-recorder accessories; one hundred and eight rolls of Eastman Kodak color negative film stock; sixty rolls of sound tape.

We reconfirm our plans to leave New York on Friday evening, February 17th, from Kennedy Airport, on Pan American flight No. 002; pick up the rest of the team in London; and continue our flight, arriving in India early on the morning of Sunday, February 19th.

I walk over to East Sixty-fourth Street and give all the information to the Public Relations Consul.

February 10th

"C AN YOU GET YOUR FATHER TO BOOK US INTO THE Hotel Janpath?" Bill asks over the telephone from Toronto. "Araminta knows about it, and says it's quite inexpensive. Any more static from the government?"

"No. Everything is fine. The consulate people tell me that the duty-exemption form for taking in the film stock and equipment will be waiting for us at the airport in Delhi. Our contact in Delhi, they say, is Himachal Som, of the External Affairs Ministry."

February 17th

T HE TELEPHONE RINGS IN MY OFFICE. My office assistant answers, and tells me, "The public-relations officer of Cran Productions is on the line from Toronto, wanting to know the measurements of the suitcases you and Sally are taking with you, and threatening that 'Bill will flip' if he doesn't get them immediately. Under new airline regulations, a passenger's luggage allowance is determined not by weight but by measurements."

I reach for the telephone.

"She doesn't want to talk to you," my assistant says.

"I think I should talk to her."

The public-relations officer turns out to be Araminta. "I was just trying to get some quick results," she says. "Bill doesn't want to pay excess baggage on the film stock and wants to know how much you and Sally can take as part of your luggage."

"Can't we sort that out at the airport?" Bill is flying in from Toronto this afternoon and meeting Sally and me at Kennedy.

"He says he wants to know now."

"I know, but I don't have the suitcases here with me, so I really can't help."

"O.K., but Bill is really going to flip."

When Sally and I arrive at Kennedy, around six o'clock, we find Bill standing among five large and battered Kodak cartons and looking quite flustered, for him. He is busy trying to patch up the cartons with some wide tape that is marked "Damaged," in big blue letters, every few inches. "I was looking for some tape marked 'Fragile,' but this is the only stuff the airlines seem to have," he says. "The people in Boston did such a rotten packing job that we're lucky I got it this far."

I introduce Sally to him. He gives her a peremptory nod and goes back to his cartons. Sally is very pretty—she has straight strawberry-blond hair and blue eyes—and I sense that she is a little miffed at Bill's inattentiveness.

"I've been carting this stuff around this bloody airport ever since my plane landed, four hours ago," he says. "The airline people wouldn't have anything to do with it until our check-in-time."

Sally and I are able to check one carton each as part of our luggage. Bill checks two as part of his, and he has to pay an eighty-five-dollar excess-baggage charge for the fifth.

"I suppose the production budget can stand that," he says, with a laugh.

Sally and I arrange to sit together and ask Bill to join us, but he says firmly that he would prefer to sit by himself and read John le Carré's "The Honourable Schoolboy." I notice a new formality in Bill—as if Sally's presence were a bar to the intimate Oxford manner he had assumed at previous meetings.

February 18th

I N LONDON, SALLY AND I COME UPON BILL wandering around inside Heathrow Airport, pipe in hand. "Didn't you hear the announcement that passengers aren't supposed to leave the aircraft, because of security?" he asks.

"No," Sally says. "They must have made the announcement after we left—we were almost the first ones off. So what are you doing here?"

"I slipped off just as the announcement was being made," Bill says. "I can't find the crew. I hope to God they haven't gone to some other airline. I told Ivan distinctly we were flying Pan Am."

We walk up and down endless corridors looking for the crew. I imagine the three crew members' arriving in Delhi by themselves and having their equipment confiscated, and my having to run around and being told by an endless stream of officials, "We can do nothing now that a file has been started." But Bill appears unperturbed, as if he were trying to show himself equal to a crisis. He flips through a stack of paperbacks at a newsstand and finally buys a couple of Agatha Christie mysteries, saying, "This should keep me amused until India."

Our flight is announced, and we go to the boarding gate. Suddenly, Bill shouts "There they are!" and runs up to two men and a woman sitting in a corner of the boarding lounge. Bill and the two men—Ivan Strasburg and Eoin McCann—fall on each other like lodge brothers who haven't met in years.

Ivan Strasburg is a strong, wiry, handsome man in his mid-thirties, with slightly curly black hair and a black beard flecked with gray, who is well tanned and radiates good health and good cheer. He is dressed in a black linen safari jacket, bluejeans, a denim shirt, and sensible walking shoes, and gives the impression of having knocked about in far regions and gone on hard climbs. In style and dress, Eoin (pronounced "Owen") McCann could pass for a somewhat older, slightly eccentric Ivan. A man of medium height with a round head, short silvery-gray hair, a silvery-white, closely trimmed beard, and intense grayish-green eyes, he is wearing a green corduroy jacket, a green sweatshirt, and tight bluejeans turned up to show his boots. Pinned to his sweatshirt is a green plastic elephant; around his neck is a black muffler with shiny silver stripes; and on his little finger is a large silver ring. He speaks with an Irish lilt. The woman, introduced as Jane Jackson, the camera assistant, is thin, long-boned, and energetic-looking, probably in her late twenties, with slightly wavy mouse-brown hair cut very short, suggesting a skinhead who has allowed her hair to grow out a bit. She wears plain brown-rimmed glasses and no makeup. She is dressed in jeans and a T-shirt.

"There is this fabulous old geezer who works as an errand boy for a chemist," Bill is saying animatedly to the crew. "He takes medicine and bandages to the halt, the lame, and the blind."

As Bill draws a more and more fanciful character sketch of Chachaji, the crew members grow more and more skeptical. They are amazed that we have no script, no story—just some poor, eighty-three-year-old man. "It sounds like a nice short for the World Health Organization," Ivan says. "I don't suppose he's ever seen a motion-picture camera. I hope we won't scare him."

February 19th

CUSTOMS OFFICIALS AT THE AIRPORT DENY ALL knowledge of the promised duty-exemption form—and, for that matter, of our coming. They say that we must immediately "reëxport" the film stock and equipment or they will impound it. It is the middle of the night and it is Sunday. All government offices are closed. (Indians by and large observe the Christian sabbath—a holdover from British times.) Bill, Sally, and I have been travelling almost continuously for nearly twenty-four hours. Except for our little illegal leg-stretching in London, we have not been off the plane. Because of the time change, we have lost ten and a half hours. Ivan has been cradling the camera in his lap and Eoin the tape recorder in his. Everyone has reason to be tired, but no one seems the slightest bit disconcerted; it is as if such slipups by government departments and such threats from customs officers were a normal part of location work. I go from customs official to higher customs official, explaining our project, until I am presented to a sympathetic Punjabi, who lets the film stock and the equipment into the country on condition that we leave with him a complete inventory in sextuplicate and that I appear in person Monday morning with a duly executed duty-exemption form.

Ivan, as if he had foreseen the request for multiple copies of the inventory, hands over a sheaf of them, typed on his stationery. We are then given formal permission to take the film stock and the equipment with us to our hotel.

Outside the customs enclosure, my mother—Mamaji, as we call her, in Indian English—and my youngest sister, Usha, who ordinarily lives in Kalamazoo, Michigan, but is here at present, staying with our parents, are waiting to greet us. They tell me that at nine o'clock this morning there is to be a prenuptial ceremony at my sister Nimi's house for Rajani, the bride.

"Would your friends like to photograph it?" Mamaji asks.

I call Bill over and ask him.

"It's always good public relations to give the crew a couple of days' rest," he says. "Even if Chacha himself were getting married in the morning, I couldn't call the crew."

❦

HOURS LATER, I WAKE UP from a sound sleep in my room at the Janpath Hotel. It is around eleven, and I go down to the coffee shop—just across from the reception desk—where all of us have agreed to meet for breakfast. The others are there, but it seems that none of them have slept very well. Each has changed rooms at least twice, because the air-conditioning didn't work, because the room looked out onto a wall, because there were centipedes dropping from the ceiling or lizards crawling in the bathtub. Bill still manages to seem cheerful, but some of the crew's skepticism may have got to him. "Will old Chacha visually add up to anything?" he demands of me.

"Why don't we go across and meet him? Then you can judge for yourself," I say.

"Would Sahib like another *samosa?*" a bearer asks. (A *samosa* is a fried stuffed pastry.)

"Sahib would," Bill says, and then, to me, "Chacha can wait. Cran Sahib didn't sleep a wink last night."

Everyone laughs, Bill loudest of all. The tenser Bill is, the louder he laughs.

February 20th

B ILL COMES DOWN TO THE COFFEE SHOP FOR BREAK-
fast looking relaxed and expensive. He plunks
down on the table a copy of Suetonius's "De
Vita Caesarum," in Latin, and regales Ivan
with a juicy bit of gossip from ancient Rome,
which I miss, because just then the bearer asks
me, in Punjabi, for my order.

"Suetonius is marvellous bedtime reading," Bill
says. "Compared to those emperors, Nixon was a babe
in the woods. I was thinking in my bath, What would
old Chacha make of Suetonius?"

"Who knows?" I say. "But why don't we at least
go and meet him?"

"Chacha will keep," Bill says, getting up and going
across to the reception desk.

I have by now suggested many times to Bill that
we go and meet Chachaji, but each time he has put me
off. Is he afraid that Chachaji won't work out and we
may not have a film?

"This is one hell of a way to produce a film," Eoin
says. "I don't think I've ever been on a film unit on
which the producer hasn't spent so much as an hour on
location preparing for the film and doesn't have a line
of script."

"I think it's very brave of Bill to run the risk of
doing a film this way," I say.

Ivan discreetly changes the subject. "We can't do

anything until I've arranged for extra lighting cables and some Indian-type plugs," he says.

Apparently, lighting cables are very heavy, and the crew didn't know exactly what kind of plugs they would need, but someone in the business told Bill about a man named Prem Prakash, who works for Visnews—an international news-film agency—in Delhi, and who has helped foreign television crews obtain such accessories in the past. Ivan and Jane go out in search of Prem Prakash, and Eoin goes up to his room to read.

Bill comes back, and says, "I think I have found a good shipping agent for the exposed film. The ABC and BBC people use him."

"But we haven't shot anything yet," Sally says.

"Before I expose a foot of film, I have to make sure that I have a reliable shipping agent," Bill says. "I knew a producer once who placed his shipment in the hands of an unreliable agent. The customs people X-rayed it and turned beautiful orange sunsets bright green. You can't imagine what can go wrong between shooting on location and seeing the rushes back home. The plane carrying our film could crash or be hijacked. The WGBH people could dillydally in Boston about getting the film on a bus to New York, where the best laboratories are. And even the best laboratories can slip up—scratch the negative, or lose a shot, especially if it is at the end of a roll. Anywhere along the way, film can be mislaid or damaged. It's a nerve-racking business."

The government offices are open now, and Bill, Sally, and I rush over to the External Affairs Ministry to sort out the duty-exemption form with our contact, Himachal Som. Som's office is overflowing with foreigners needing his help, and Som, conducting several conversations at once, has the air of a traffic policeman. He seems to be an obliging man, who likes to give only good news. Over the clatter of a teletype machine, he is saying, "Yes, yes. . . . I will try. . . . Certainly. . . . I will apply for the permission for you. . . . It shall be done."

Som offers everyone coffee or tea, asking each person how he would like it, but by the time it arrives the person in question has usually gone. Occasionally, he summons his personal assistant—or P.A., as such an assistant is called here—and tells him to "do the needful" or dictates a letter. Whether "the needful" ever gets done or the letter typed and signed, it is hard to say.

We eventually get a duty-exemption form from Som and take it out to the airport, where an endless series of customs officials put their stamps and signatures on it. At last, the stock and equipment, which are actually lying in our hotel rooms, are officially deemed admitted into the country.

Back at the hotel, Bill decides to go off in search of a big American station wagon with good suspension, which can take the crew and all the equipment and can also be used for tracking shots. "I wonder if you can find a bloody American car in this blighted place," he says. "How do I say 'tailgate' and 'suspension' in Hindi?"

I offer to go with him, but he tells me, "Go and limber up Chacha and prepare him for the assault."

"Why don't you come with me?" I ask, trying once again to corral Bill into meeting Chachaji.

"I think I should see to the station wagon first. If

Chacha's going to be the superstar of our film, we want to take him for a ride, don't we?" He laughs at his own joke.

DADDYJI—AS WE CALL MY FATHER—likes to have his elevenses with any and all members of the family at Gaylord's, an upper-middle-class, air-conditioned restaurant in Connaught Circus, in the centre of New Delhi. The restaurant is known for its coffee with ice cream and for its chicken patties—favorite refreshments here.

"Where is Chachaji?" I ask, joining the family at Gaylord's after telephoning Mamaji and Daddyji to ask them to bring him.

"I asked him to come with us," Daddyji says. "But he said, 'Just give me the money for the chicken patty and ice-cream coffee. I am saving up for a pair of shoes.' So I gave him the money."

"He's very shrewd," Mamaji says. "He couldn't have come anyway. He has to go to work."

TONIGHT IS THE FIRST OF THE TRADITIONAL three evenings of singing and dancing leading up to Rajani's wedding. I suggest to Bill that the singsong, as such an evening is called, would make a good sequence. "If we do the Chachaji story, we have to do the family, and if we do the family, what could be more central to it than a wedding? It would also be a good way of introducing the crew to the family and getting some Indian music on the soundtrack."

"I still haven't found a station wagon," Bill says. "All the same, I'll come and case the joint with you. But the crew should be left to their own devices this evening. It's always bad public relations to make them work hard right away." If Bill is still worried about the revolt of those idle soldiers, he shows no sign of it.

On our way out of the hotel, we bump into the crew. Ivan and Jane say they have spent the entire day looking for Prem Prakash and the essential cables and Indian plugs. Prem Prakash was never where he was supposed to be.

"Hey! Have you written the story yet? Why don't you call it 'Six Characters in Search of a Film'?" Ivan asks me facetiously.

"Do you have any idea of what we'll be filming?" Eoin asks. "I've started my shooting-log cards, but so far the only information I have is technical stuff they'll need back home to synchronize sound with picture."

I am encouraged by this small, if technical, start.

February 21st

"ARE WE SHOOTING TODAY?" IVAN ASKS BILL OVER breakfast.

"Not in the daytime, at least," Bill says. "But if I find a station wagon, it could be singsong tonight. You chaps had better keep after Prem Prakash. We can't do anything without proper Indian plugs and ropes, now, can we?"

"What's the name of the hotel almost next door to us?" Eoin asks me as we finish breakfast.

"The Imperial," I say.

"It has a swimming pool," he says.

"Is the Delhi water safe to swim in?" Sally asks.

"It depends," I say. "The Imperial is known to have a pretty good filter system."

Eoin, Ivan, and Jane, with Sally close behind, rush upstairs for swimsuits, calling back that we should all meet at the Imperial's outdoor café for a late tandoori lunch.

As Bill once more goes in search of a station wagon, I rent for Sally and me a modest but quite roomy cream-colored Ambassador with gray trim—a shorter, Indian-made version of a standard English car. I also arrange for a driver I know to take us around. He has a government job as a driver, from which he usually takes a "casual leave" when I am in Delhi, so that he can work for me. He is a large, tireless, jovial, irreverent Sikh, about six feet tall, named Yoginder

Singh. He boasts that in his government job he has never driven for anyone less than a Department Secretary or Minister, and he takes pride in always being where he is wanted when he is wanted, no matter what the weather is, where his car is parked, or how long he has been kept waiting. There is something at once dignified and flamboyant about him. I am especially pleased to have him this time, because he has a natural authority, which should prove useful in controlling the crowds that always gather here at the sight of a camera or a tape recorder, and because I know he will enter into the spirit of our project and be generally helpful.

As I am talking to Yoginder Singh on the steps of the hotel, Bill arrives in a big old yellow American Ford station wagon—the kind of expensive-looking car that only embassies and tourist organizations can afford to run here. It is driven by another Sikh, who could pass for Yoginder Singh's brother, except that he is unsmiling, even dour.

Bill, who has heard that "Orientals" are always out to cheat Westerners, calls on me to negotiate the rates with his driver.

"He's O.K., Ved Sahib," Yoginder Singh says. "He belongs to my temple."

The new driver, Amarjit Singh, is quite agreeable to my rates. I ask him if he can speak any English.

"Ved Sahib, he doesn't have to," Yoginder Singh puts in. "My car will always be in the front, and I will make sure he follows."

"Good show!" Bill exclaims when I interpret for him. (Yoginder Singh himself speaks only a little En-

glish; his language, like that of most Sikhs, is Punjabi.)
"Yoginder Singh is going to be a real asset. I will ride
in your Ambassador, and lead with Yoginder Singh."

The Imperial Hotel serves us a marvellous lunch.
Ivan, Eoin, and Bill are able to put away extraordinary
amounts of food. Prem Prakash has still not been
found, and Ivan can't stop talking about him. He im-
agines Prem Prakash sitting on a hoard of cables and
plugs in Calcutta or Bombay, and surfacing in New
Delhi only when we are ready to leave. As Ivan talks,
the elusive Prem Prakash becomes at once an eccentric,
if absent, member of our team and a malevolent force
toying with the fate of our project.

Overhead, kites cry. I eat quickly, and tell everyone
about a kite that once swooped down and snatched a
chapatti from my hand, almost taking a finger with it.

After lunch, Ivan, Eoin, and Jane go off to look for
Prem Prakash again, this time in the station wagon.
Bill, Sally, and I go in the Ambassador to look for
Chachaji—at last. No one in the family knows the
exact name or address of Chachaji's place of work.
(Everyone in India has so many poor relations that the
general principle is to stand ready to rescue them in
illness or any other emergency, give them little bits of
money, and do some strategic string-pulling to help
them obtain jobs and places to live, but not get involved
beyond that—a principle that the poor relations grasp
even more firmly than those who formulated it, since
their lives depend on it.)

Our first stop is in Bhogal Bazaar, at a modest
electrical shop owned by Dalip Singh, a middle-aged
nephew of Chachaji's, who is likely to know Chachaji's

whereabouts. Dalip himself had been a poor relation for most of his life, but now, thanks to a recent upsurge of building in New Delhi, he is a well-to-do contractor. He is not at his shop, but his wife, Mehma, is, and over tea and sweetmeats she tells us that the chemical-supply store where Chachaji works is on the other side of Bhogal Bazaar. We drive there.

The store turns out to be a typical, if dilapidated, New Delhi house—a compact, low structure of brick and cement with a small courtyard and a veranda. A signboard by the gate has "The Pharmacy of Prosperity" written on it. Just inside the gate to the courtyard is Chachaji. He sits nodding in the sun in an old straight-backed chair behind a couple of wooden crates, which serve as his desk. On top of the crates are a large work ledger and his public badge of dignity—a bright-pink turban. His clothes—hand-me-downs, which he has always called "my borrowed feathers"—are shabby and hang on him like rags on a scarecrow. He has a round, bald head and a pointed face with a pencil-line mustache, but the most noticeable thing about him is his leathery skin, which is stretched so taut on his face and head that it accentuates the sharpness of his features and makes his eyes and cheekbones stand out. He is astonishingly fair for an Indian, and there is a touch of the natural sahib about him. His eyes are blue—something very rare here, too—and though he is eighty-three, his vision is so good that he doesn't need glasses.

At the sight of him, Bill explodes into laughter. "Visually, he's great!" he exclaims. "Couldn't be better!"

We get out of the car, and I call out a greeting to Chachaji. He squints, and slowly puts on his turban.

"My God!" Bill whispers. "He looks like an ancient turtle! And that pink turban!"

Chachaji stands up and shuffles out through the gate toward us, taking little, cautious steps, as if he were afraid that the ground underfoot might suddenly give way. "You should have sent me a message, and I would have called on you," he says. "This is not a fit place for gentlemen." He has a thin, whining voice, which sometimes croaks.

We stand and talk for a while. "The owners of the establishment—Chopra Sahib and Young Chopra Sahib—are both away," he says, in Punjabi, and I interpret. "They always lock the house and take the keys. This is no place to entertain my fortunate relation and sympathetic benefactors."

I remind him that we are going to make a film about him.

"Chopra Sahib and Young Chopra Sahib are not handsome enough for foreign photographs," Chachaji says. "They are not gentlemen."

"Will you be at the singsong tonight?" I ask him.

"Such auspicious occasions should never be missed," he says.

On the ride back to the hotel, I ask Bill if we can start filming the singsong that night. He had stopped by with me at the singsong yesterday evening, but he had stayed only a few minutes, leaving before Chachaji and many of the other guests arrived.

"I can't see the point of filming it, but O.K.," he says. "Let's do it as a practice session, to break the ice. We have to begin somewhere. All those sensuous women will make a great picture."

At the hotel, Ivan announces that he has got the cables and plugs. "We finally found that bloke, actually sitting in a chair."

"We're in business!" Bill exclaims. "Let's have a dry run tonight and film the wretched singsong. 'Chacha' must essentially be a film about the family, and what is more central to a family than a wedding?" Bill, I have come to realize, often changes his mind.

I'M NOT SURE HOW MY SISTER Nimi and her husband, Mahesh, will react to the idea of our filming one of the most intimate moments in family life—their daughter's singsong. I phone them to ask, bracing myself for an argument. To my surprise, they agree, without hesitation and without any restrictions. Either the novelty of the idea appeals to them or my involvement with the film reassures them.

So this evening we set out in a little cavalcade in search of Chachaji and our film—Bill, Sally, and I in the Ambassador, with Ivan, Eoin, and Jane in the station wagon behind.

At my sister's house, which is a spacious government residence, many members of my family and many of Nimi's and Mahesh's close friends have gathered in the drawing room for the singsong—the women mostly sitting on the floor, and the men reclining in armchairs, perching on stools, or just standing around. My parents are sitting together on a divan and look very happy. They have been married for fifty-two years and have sixteen grandchildren. Rajani is the fourth grandchild to be married.

Chachaji, as the oldest relative present, sits with my parents. He coughs occasionally, but tries to make himself inconspicuous. When I introduce the crew to him, he makes no attempt to learn their names, and thereafter he simply refers to all of them as "Vedji's party."

The women, who are wearing their best clothes and jewelry, start clapping and singing bits and pieces of Punjabi folk songs, joking, jumping up and dancing, laughing, crying. There are a lot of starts and stops. Finally, a pretty young woman with huge dark eyes—a singer on All India Radio—takes charge. She sits down at a two-sided drum and beats out a rhythm while another young woman sits across from her tapping the drum cylinder with a spoon in almost metronomic accompaniment. The drummer sings as she plays, leading the women in a medley of songs, suggestively coy and teasingly sexual, which coach the bride in the conduct of the marital bed even as they embarrass her. Rajani arranges and rearranges her sari and tries to look grown up, but no one pays much attention to her, because she is only an excuse for the married women to remember themselves as innocent brides.

Bill looks relaxed and donnish, with his pipe in one hand and a glass of beer in the other. He and Ivan move about the room quietly discussing "wide shots" and "tight shots," their voices a sort of undertone to the singing and the conversations around them. Eoin, Jane, and Sally busy themselves checking lights and power outlets, positioning microphones, pushing cables out of the way. Eoin seems oblivious of the fact that he has a bulky tape recorder hanging at his hip. He wanders around with a book of Hemingway stories in one hand and reads when he has nothing else to do. Once the equipment has been set up, Jane clumps after Ivan, the pockets of her overalls bulging with screwdrivers, brushes, plugs, and pieces of chalk. Over her shoulder she has a large canvas bag from which protrude a small, squarish board with a clapper and a numerical register, many pens and pencils and pieces of chalk, and various camera accessories. Sally is very ladylike, and quickly establishes a rapport with the family, which is useful in helping everyone forget the presence of the filming paraphernalia. The crew all weave in and out among family and guests with astonishing ease. They are so casually, almost scruffily, dressed that they are accepted good-naturedly as bumbling amateurs making a home movie.

"I don't see the point of filming this chaos," Ivan says, half seriously, as shooting is about to start. "I thought you told me we were going to film an old man. Here we are filming the pride of India." He is lying on the floor ready to take the opening shot.

Bill laughs. "That's a nice shot of the women singing," he says, looking through the viewfinder. He calls out "Board!"

Jane whips out the board and quickly sets the numerical register:

Roll 1
Take 1

She holds up the board, with the clapper opened at an angle, in front of the camera. Ivan starts the camera and Eoin the tape recorder. Jane drops the clapper and moves out of range. Shooting is under way.

Bill calls out "Cut!" and shooting stops.

A few moments later, Ivan is on the other side of the room for the next take. His camera weighs about twenty-five pounds, but he carries it lightly. It seems like an extension of his body, although he is occasionally heard to mutter, "Camera is cruel to old men." He is scarcely thirty-five.

"Get that bored-looking man in the armchair puffing a pipe," Bill tells Ivan.

Ivan turns the camera on the man in question, who, from his expression, might be at a dreary office meeting rather than in a room filled with lovely women singing songs that would send most men's hearts racing. He's a perfect foil for the singsong.

After some more shooting of the singsong, Bill, Ivan, Eoin, and Jane go out to take some shots of the exterior of the house.

At the end of the evening, back at the hotel, Eoin goes over the log for all the shooting:

TAPE ROLL I

sync (film roll 1, take 1, front board) *women sing at party*

sync (film roll 2, take 1, end board) same as above

(film roll 2, take 2, mute)

(film roll 2, take 3) no good

(film roll 3, take 1, front board) no good

sync (film roll 3, take 2, end board) *three girls enter house* (night exterior)

sync (film roll 3, take 3, end board) same as above

Eoin explains to me that the log will be used back

in Boston to synchronize his sound with Ivan's film. "Front board" and "end board" refer to the placement of the clapper board at the beginning or the end of a shot, or "take." When there is enough time to line up a take, the board goes at the beginning, but when the camera catches a quick, spontaneous action and there is no time to call for the board, it goes at the end. "Mute" refers to a take without sound. "No good" refers to a take that for technical or other reasons is deemed unusable.

"Where is Chachaji in all this?" I ask.

"He's in there, all right," Bill says. "Just doesn't get lead billing for the moment."

CHACHAJI, MY FATHER'S FIRST COUSIN, whose real name is Bahali Ram, was born in a little village called Nabipur Piran, in the Lahore District, in the British Punjab, on or about the fifteenth of March, 1895. In the seventeenth century, the village and its land had belonged to the Moghul Emperor Aurangzeb, who deeded it to the Pirs, or hereditary Muslim religious leaders, in the region, so by Chachaji's time most of the land and the houses in the village belonged to Muslims. Because of its Moghul past, the village was well off. "There was no shortage of cereal and lentils in my village," Chachaji says. "Practically every family kept a cow or a buffalo. You could drink milk from morning to evening and there would still be more to drink."

Chachaji's father, Jawahar Mal, who was one of the few Hindus in the village, was a humble shopkeeper, selling farm produce and ghi. His main pastime was smoking a hubble-bubble. Chachaji's mother, who was my father's aunt Ganga Devi, was known as the prettiest of the Hindu women in the village. "She used to grind fresh flour on the millstones with her own hands every day," Chachaji says. "Every night, she would wrap the leftover *parathas* [triangles of un-leavened fried bread] she had made in moist cheese-cloth, and we would eat them in the morning, by which time the *parathas* were so soft that they would melt in your mouth like butter. But she would still put more butter on them. Her kitchen was always overflowing with ghi, lentils, potatoes, and peas. Everything was first-class. And it was all for us."

When Chachaji was about nine years old, his mother was stricken by plague. As she was dying, she called her husband to her side and made him promise that he would never remarry. He respected her last wish, even though it meant raising seven young chil-dren—four boys and three girls—by himself. (By the time Chachaji was twenty-one, two of his brothers and two of his sisters had died.)

When Chachaji was eight, he started going to school, in a one-room wattle-and-daub building that also served as the office of the only government official in the village, who was known as "the man with the white horse." The school had one teacher, a mullah; one Urdu book, for all classes; and five students. Cha-chaji studied there off and on for several years. When he was about twelve, he and two fellow-students were selected to go to Sharakpur—a subdistrict headquarters, a day's walk from the village—and sit for a scholarship examination to get into the vernacular middle school (the equivalent of junior high school) there. "We left at seven o'clock in the morning, in the company of our teacher," Chachaji recalls. "He had a beard and rode on a pony. We boys walked. We walked for twelve hours. It started getting dark. We were tired and hungry. Our teacher stopped in a Muslim hamlet, and he and the two other boys, who were Muslims, went inside for food. I was left standing outside. In those days, a Hindu could not partake of the food of a Muslim. The little food I'd brought with me from the village I had long since finished. The Muslim woman came out of the house and, taking pity on me, offered me half a kilo of milk with sugar in it. I couldn't resist. I shut my eyes, said the name of the Hindu god, and quickly drank down the milk."

It seems that about a hundred boys, from villages all over the district, sat for the examination at Sharakpur, for four government scholarships. "Right at the start, I walked up to the examiner and told him, as a ruse, that I was a little hard of hearing, and suggested that when he was asking questions or giving dictation he should stand near my desk and speak loudly," Chachaji says. "The first part of the examination was sums. He looked at our answers there and then, and immediately eliminated sixty boys. The next question concerned the reign of Emperor Akbar. He eliminated twenty-five more boys, including the two Muslim boys from my village. The examiner must have liked my forthright manner, because I got one of the scholarships. When I came back home, it was as if the entire village had been set on fire. A man from a neighboring village came on his horse and asked me, 'How did you do it?' 'With a lot of *parathas,* chapattis, butter, ghi, yogurt, and buttermilk,' I said. That night, my family fêted me with dishes of sweetened rice, turmeric balls in yogurt, and other delicacies. On that day, I could have had anything I asked for to eat or drink."

Chachaji spent the next three years in the vernacular middle school in Sharakpur, where the medium of instruction was Urdu, as it had been in his village school. "I still remember that within my scholarship of two rupees a month I was comfortably able to meet all my expenses for board, lodging, fees, books, and such things," he says. "You will say this is impossible. But in that era you could buy two and a half pounds of ghi for one rupee. In this era, one pound of good ghi will cost you nearly eight rupees."

Chachaji went as far as he could with his studies at Sharakpur—to the eighth standard—and then moved to Lahore, the capital of the Punjab, where he lived with my grandfather's younger brother, Bhaji Ganga Ram, who was the first university graduate in the family's history. Bhaji Ganga Ram took under his wing practically all his teen-age nephews, including my father, as they became ready for higher education—until my grandfather, Lalaji, himself moved to Lahore. In Lahore, Chachaji's classes would be conducted in English, so Bhaji Ganga Ram put him in a special school for teaching English to village boys, and Chachaji spent two years there. He says, however, "English is Mount Everest and I'm no mountain climber." Indeed, Chachaji's English remained very poor. His accent was so rustic that when he spoke English, people thought he was speaking gibberish. He decided he didn't want to go on with his studies, so Lalaji—who was by then living in Lahore—got him a job as an apprentice to a petty official. Chachaji recalls, "My first day on the job, I had to ride a horse and take two bundles of fodder to my employer's house. As I was riding along, a tonga-wallah came up behind me and created a disturbance. My horse bolted, and I found myself on the road with the fodder spilled all over me. A policeman appeared. 'Clear the road of fodder!' he shouted. 'Mr. Policeman,' I said. 'Look at me. I am a small, weak fellow who in one stroke has lost his horse and maybe his job. Do I look like the kind of fellow who could do such heavy work? Give me a courteous hand.' The policeman began barking at me. Luckily, a hill fellow, who was used to controlling wild horses, appeared with my horse. He bundled up the fodder and sent me on my way. When I'd gone hardly a quarter of a mile, the horse threw me and the fodder a second time. I decided I would never get on a horse again. I went home on foot, without the fodder; I fortified myself with food and milk; and I quietly ran back to my village."

Lalaji visited the village and took Chachaji back to Lahore. He forced Chachaji to go back to school. Chachaji then spent two years preparing for his matriculation, or school-leaving, examination, but when the time came to sit for it, he balked. Lalaji caught Chachaji by the back of his neck, marched him to the university examination hall, and pushed him inside the door, saying, "Pass or fail, you must sit for the examination—and see that you don't fail!" Chachaji managed· to scrape through, and thereafter he nearly always wrote "Matric Passed" after his name.

Chachaji applied for a job as a clerk-accountant for a local honey dealer who had a stall *cum* office in the bazaar. He got the job, but within fifteen days he lost it, because he ate too much of the honey. Over the next few years, he did many odd jobs, and even taught school for a short while, but no job quite suited him. (As a schoolteacher, he was intimidated by boys of twelve who were taller than he was.)

In 1922, Chachaji's father died, and his younger brother Kidar Nath took over their father's little shop, because, Chachaji says, "I had no head for business." From then on, he became the family's poor relation— "the least and the last," as the rest of the family called him.

Around 1922, Daulat Ram, my father's younger brother, became a public-health officer for the Lahore and Sheikhupura Districts—in Chachaji's words, "the king of two districts." The "king" made Chachaji a "plague supervisor." He was given a donkey for travel, two peons to accompany him, and a supply of rattraps and rat poison. His instructions were to go from village to village, kill rats, and bring back as many rattails as he could, in proof of his work. It was the first job that Chachaji had really enjoyed, because wherever he and his peons went they were fêted; and Chachaji took great pride in collecting, counting, re-counting, and re-cording in a government file the number of rattails that his team had snipped off—with a pair of "Made in England" shears.

In 1924, Daulat Ram was transferred to Rawalpindi. His successor had his own poor relations to take
care of, and dismissed Chachaji, whereupon Chachaji
and his wife, Tara (he had married two years earlier),
headed for Rawalpindi. Daulat Ram got the clerk he
had inherited moved to some other office and gave
Chachaji the job—a step up for Chachaji. Daulat Ram
was transferred again three years later, but Chachaji
stayed where he was, because by then Daulat Ram was
so well placed in the Department of Public Health
that no one would dare dismiss his first cousin. Eventually, Chachaji became head clerk, with a salary of a
hundred and fifty rupees a month. He bought a plot of
land and built on it a small two-room house, which,
unlike the house in which he was born and grew up,
was a permanent structure of brick and cement. And
there, in 1932, his first child—a boy, whom he named
Madan—was born.

One day not long afterward, Chachaji came home
from the office and saw standing in front of his wife's
full-length looking glass a Sikh gentleman, tying his
turban. The Sikh was as tall, handsome, and muscular
as Chachaji was short, plain, and thin.

"Who are you?" Chachaji asked meekly, as if he,
rather than the Sikh, were the intruder.

"Speak up," the Sikh said. "You know me. I'm
Avtar Singh. I am going to be your lodger."

Chachaji then remembered that he and Tara had
met the fellow a few months earlier, when they happened to wander into a political rally against the British. The Sikh had struck up a conversation with Tara,
who was as saucy as she was pretty.

Chachaji as a Young Man

The Sikh now moved into the cramped little house, because that was what Tara wanted. Tara had such a hot temper that Chachaji was afraid of her and dared not object. Whenever he did cautiously broach the subject of living without their lodger, Tara would say, "He is an aristocrat, from a landed family—a Sirdarji. He's doing you a favor by staying with you. If you don't like him, you go." Chachaji felt he could do nothing—particularly since he had put the house in Tara's name.

"I am a trusting soul," Chachaji says. "While I was typing away at the office to keep the home fires burning, the Sirdarji did his mischief. He moved not only into the house but also into my wife's heart. Tell me, what could I have done? She had taken a fancy to him, and I never stopped fancying her."

Tara had four children altogether—a second son, Ravinder, and two daughters, Kamla and Mohini. Chachaji, Tara, the children, and the Sirdarji all lived together until the Partition of India, in 1947, when Tara, the children, and the Sirdarji fled to India and settled in Delhi, leaving Chachaji to guard the house.

"She said 'Ta-ta' and went," Chachaji says. "What good was the house to me? As some poet has said,

> This house is neither yours nor mine.
> In the end, only birds will live in it."

Chachaji was one of the last Hindus to leave Rawalpindi. A kind Muslim driver hid him under some big burlap bags of lentils he was carrying in his lorry, and took him to a refugee camp in the village of Wah, where other Hindu refugees were waiting to be evacuated from Pakistan to India. At one point, the lorry, which was not supposed to have human cargo, was searched by Muslim soldiers. One of them slipped his hand under the bags of lentils and touched Chachaji's foot. Chachaji kept drawing his foot up and the soldier kept reaching for it. "I thought I was going to my next incarnation there and then," Chachaji says, "but the soldier must have thought that he was in contact with a rat, because he let the lorry pass."

In Wah, Chachaji finally got on one of the trains that were carrying Hindu refugees to India under military escort. "Luckily, the troops were able to fight off the Muslim mobs who attacked us on the way, and I reached Amritsar, across the border, safe and sound," Chachaji recalls. "As some poet has said,

> Henna gets its coloring from being rubbed on a stone.
> Similarly, a man gets his coloring by being rubbed up
>   against life."

In Amritsar, Chachaji continued working as a clerk for the government for a year or so, but then he reached fifty-five, the compulsory age for retirement, and was obliged to find work wherever he could—now with a member of the family, now with a small-time business. In due course, Chachaji, like other Hindu refugees, received partial compensation for lost property from the new government of independent India. He and Tara had to split the compensation, and his portion amounted to twenty-five hundred rupees. He used the money to buy living quarters in Delhi for Madan, the only child to recognize Chachaji as his father. (The other children accepted the Sirdarji as their father.) Chachaji himself made his home as a "permanent lodger" with Bhaji Ganga Ram, who at the time was the oldest surviving member of the Mehta clan and so felt obliged to take care of him.

When Bhaji Ganga Ram was dying, in 1958, he repeated to his wife, Chhoti Bhabiji, what Lalaji—head of the family until his death, in 1923—had said to him: "I'm leaving you Bahali Ram. You care for him—the least and the last of the family—and you will be caring for the family's good name." Chhoti Bhabiji and Chachaji had never got along. She used to say, "I've done so much for him I don't think I'll have to do anything for an in-law for another ten incarnations." But Chachaji felt she was not doing all she could for him, and would complain, "There is never enough ghi on the chapatti or in the lentils. And she objects if I take another spoonful."

Chhoti Bhabiji took her revenge in 1971, on her deathbed. Bhaji Ganga Ram had willed their house to the Hindu sect of Arya Samaj, with a lifetime interest to Chhoti Bhabiji. She, in turn, had the right to give Chachaji a lifetime interest in the room in which he lived, along with the use of the kitchen. My father tried to get her to perform this act of charity before her death, but she refused, saying, "I might as well leave them a resident demon."

As it turned out, the Arya Samaj couldn't evict Chachaji without lengthy and expensive court proceedings, and, besides, the members of the sect didn't want it said in the community that they had thrown an old man out of his home. So my father was able to prevail upon them to let Chachaji keep his room and use the kitchen, and they even agreed to pay him a token salary of fifteen rupees a month, in return for which Chachaji was to act as a part-time caretaker for the house in addition to continuing his regular work at the Pharmacy of Prosperity, which he had begun a year or so earlier.

February 22nd

WE PULL UP IN FRONT OF THE PHARMACY OF PROSperity at ten o'clock in the morning. Chachaji is sitting sleepily behind his crates, doing his accounts. We all go into the courtyard—all except the two drivers, who stay at the gate to keep back the crowd that gathers to see what is happening. Because the courtyard is so small, I can hear the goings on at the gate. The drivers explain in Punjabi, with a self-important air, "Sahibs have come from America and they are 'shooting.'" Both of them use the English word "shooting," speaking it as if they were impressed by the sound of it but were not quite sure what it means.

Everyone seems incredulous that so much attention is being lavished upon a poor little old man.

"Why that poor old man? Why not a healthy young celibate?" someone asks.

"They want to show Indian poverty," a young student says. "They always want to show Indian poverty."

"Chachaji, we've come here to take your picture," I say.

He seems unsure of what I mean, probably because

he thinks that only the rich get their pictures taken. When he finally seems to understand, he says, in Punjabi, "Permission must be obtained from my employers, Chopra Sahib and Young Chopra Sahib. But they are not here now." Then he goes on, in the little, whiny voice that he uses when he wants something, "I need a pair of shoes."

I translate for Bill's benefit.

"Is that what he wants?" Bill says, with a laugh. "Well, let's go and buy him some shoes. It'll make a great shot."

I tell Chachaji what we have in mind. He seems somewhat taken aback. As a rule, people just give him the money for the things he asks for, and don't help him shop—with good reason. He may spend days pricing shoes from different cobblers and bargaining with them, and eventually buy a pair of cheap shoes from a cobbler sitting in some hole in the wall. Reluctantly, he agrees to come with us in the car to Bhogal Bazaar.

Yoginder Singh, who likes to try out his little bit of English, says, "Cran Sahib, Bhogal dirty bazaar. No good for photograph." He tells me in Punjabi that we might create a riot in Bhogal Bazaar, because the moment the people there see a group of foreigners they are likely to stage a disturbance for some trumped-up reason in order to frighten the foreigners and extort money from them.

"Not when the foreigners are with Indians," I say. "Anyway, we want to film Chachaji walking in the bazaar."

We go into the bazaar with Chachaji to buy him his shoes and, at the same time, scout for locations.

The bazaar is narrow and is so crowded with pedestrians, bicycles, motorcycles, cars, bullock carts, and tongas that we can scarcely walk. Chachaji leads us into Bata's, which is the most Western-looking shop in the bazaar and a complete contrast to the string of colorful, cramped stalls all around. Chachaji hesitates. I realize that he may never have entered such a shop before. There is hardly a shoe in the shop—men's or women's—to fit him. The smallest pair of men's shoes, size 6, which the salesman presses on him, is too large for him, and he complains that the shoes are in any case too stiff, too leathery, too bulky—too intimidating. He has grown used to wearing women's shoes, which are softer and lighter. Yet the largest pair of women's shoes, size 5, is too loose and the next-largest, size 4, is too tight. At the moment, he is wearing an old, stretched pair of size 4s that belonged to my mother, and he says he wants a pair like them. The salesman cannot oblige him, so Chachaji, afraid of losing his chance for a new pair of shoes, asks the salesman to wrap up the most expensive pair of men's size 6 he has tried on.

"Shooting this shop would be a complete mistake," Bill says, paying for the shoes. "Now let's try to get some real local color."

Eoin starts taping bazaar sounds, and Ivan starts shooting Chachaji walking—or, rather, shuffling and weaving—through the bazaar, but cannot keep up with him, because crowds are milling around trying to see and touch the camera. Though India has one of the largest film industries in the world, the processes of filming and recording are largely restricted to studios and are still alien and magical to most people.

"I'd like to murder the whole lot of them," Bill says. "The working conditions here are terrible. In England, I could have done the bloody walk in one minute flat. Here, at this rate, we'll be at it for the whole day. Get Chacha, and let's forget about the bloody walk for now. Ivan, why don't you go off and try some mute random shots of bazaar types while Eoin distracts the mob with the tape recorder. Meet us at the car in fifteen minutes." Following Bill's suggestion, Ivan disappears into the crowd while Eoin diverts it by taping some "wild track"—sound not recorded simultaneously with specific shots.

When we are all in the car again, Eoin enters in his shooting log:

TAPE ROLL I
(wild track) sounds of the market
sync (film roll 3, take 4, front board) *Chacha walks through market*
TAPE ROLL 2
(film roll 4, take 2, mute) daytime

Back at the Pharmacy of Prosperity, as we are entering the shop, which is now open, Chachaji says loudly, so that he can be heard inside, "You should take the photographs of Chopra Sahib and Young Chopra Sahib. They are real gentlemen."

The older Chopra is away, but his son, a friendly-looking Punjabi, can't take his eyes off our camera and tape recorder.

I explain our project to him while Bill and Ivan look around.

The inside of the shop is tiny and so cluttered up

with a desk, a typewriter, a table, and a couple of chairs, and with cartons, tins, and bottles—piled up on the floor and on shelves—that there is hardly room for us. The place smells stale and dusty, and several toothless people stare at us from the back yard.

"I have no objection to being photographed," young Chopra says. "But you must include my father in one of the photographs, and you must send me copies." He walks to the back door, beyond which a demented-looking man is standing at a tub out in the open, washing some bottles and scrubbing off their labels.

"Hey, that bottle washer is a terrific scene setter!" Bill says. "Let's get some shots of him. He'll do fine for the tawdriness of the place."

Young Chopra becomes a little edgy. "He doesn't work here full time," he says. "You take your photograph of me at this desk."

I begin to negotiate with him about taking a shot of the bottle washer, too.

Bill whispers to me, "What the hell! The shop looks crummy enough. An inside shot will do fine, and we can include the Chopra fellow and his desk or not, as we like. He'll never know the difference. Let's set up."

Young Chopra orders the bottle washer to leave off his work and to replace Chachaji's crates with a table. The bottle washer picks up an old, beat-up square table and walks toward the front of the shop.

"No, no, no!" Bill shouts, catching on. "We want to take a picture of Chacha sitting at those crates." He turns to me and says under his breath, "Curse Chopra.

The crates are so much nicer. Can you try to get him to leave them alone?"

Young Chopra, however, is adamant. "Bahali Ram always sits at the table," he says. "Don't you, Bahali Ram?"

"We saw him sitting at the crates earlier," Bill says.

Chachaji looks a bit confused, and then says shrewdly, "Accounts can only be done properly on a table." In the meantime, the bottle washer has replaced the crates with the table.

The older Chopra comes in. He's a sly, suspicious-looking man with discolored, jagged teeth, who bristles at our presence. (The identities of Chopra and young Chopra have been disguised here.) He questions me closely in Punjabi, and I reassure him that we have no ulterior motives and just want realistic pictures of Chachaji. He asks me the particulars of my caste and family, and when I tell him he becomes somewhat less unfriendly. He tells me how he sends Chachaji out on errands, and I translate for Bill.

"Tell Daddy Chopra to push open the screen door and summon Chacha and give him an errand," Bill says. "Tell Chacha to keep on turning the pages of the ledger until he's called."

I tell Chopra and Chachaji what to do, and Bill shouts "Board!"

Chopra pushes open the screen door, as instructed, and calls out, "Lalaji, come inside. Bring ledger." ("Lalaji" is a caste title with which Chopra would not normally honor Chachaji—he would call him by his name—but then he's acting for the camera.)

Before Chopra can finish his lines, Bill yells "Cut!" Chachaji spoiled the shot by jumping up at the sound of Chopra opening the door, instead of waiting for Chopra to call him.

And so the morning goes, until we think we finally have enough good material to make a sequence of Chachaji being sent on an errand—to deliver a chemical sample to a government laboratory for testing.

Back at the hotel, Bill says, "I don't mind if we follow Chacha around for a few days, but I think he's good for only about five minutes on American TV. Maybe he could be one character in a rogue's gallery of half a dozen of your family."

"I would prefer the film to have Chachaji as its main character," I say. "It would give the film a certain unity and intensity. But what about using other members of the family to set off Chachaji?"

"How?" Bill asks.

"Film as many family occasions as we can," I say. "We could start with the bangle ceremony."

"What's that?"

"It's a Punjabi tradition for the bride's maternal uncle to put ivory bangles on the bride's wrists on her wedding day. Her father-in-law later breaks the bangles and replaces them with gold ones. No one knows any longer how the custom grew up or exactly what it means, but it probably has to do with passing the responsibility for protecting a woman from one family to another. Since I have missed the weddings of my other nieces, Nimi insists that I do my duty as maternal uncle this once, for Rajani."

"What does it involve?" Bill asks.

Chachaji at the Pharmacy of Prosperity

"Today, I have to buy the bangles. I have to go with my mother to a market in Old Delhi where the bangles are cut. Ivory is too expensive these days, so the bangle cutters use plastic."

Eoin is standing nearby, and Bill asks him what he thinks.

"It's a director's film," Eoin says.

Bill laughs. This answer has become the crew's way of saying, "The whole thing sounds peripheral, but that's Bill's problem."

"What the hell! We've got nothing better to do," Bill says.

The bangle cutter sits in front of an intricate-looking machine at a stall in a bazaar in Old Delhi. Mamaji explains to him the special reason for our visit and gives him Rajani's measurements. The bangle cutter looks at the rest of us a little uneasily but starts showing Mamaji and me his samples.

Ivan moves in behind the bangle cutter and starts shooting over his shoulder.

Mamaji is oddly silent, slightly self-conscious with my new friends. The crew's casual dress bothers her, because she thinks that people who don't take care of their appearance don't do good work. She keeps stealing glances at Jane, and I know she would love to "pretty her up." But she mostly manages to keep her attention on the bangle cutter, as she has been told to do for the camera.

The bangle cutter works on the dozen bangles we select for Rajani.

Ivan moves into the street and shoots from the front.

"I think the machine is nice," Bill says. "And it's a good Indian shot. But I don't know where I'll use it."

"It's a director's film," Ivan says.

As we are leaving, the bangle cutter shouts teasingly to Mamaji, "Mistress, I didn't recognize you today!" And they both laugh.

"We'll have our cold drink and sweetmeats next time," she says. If we hadn't been there, she would have spent a couple of hours with the bangle cutter, inquiring about his family and his business, making a social occasion out of a simple purchase.

In the Ambassador, Bill says to me, "That was pretty much a waste. An hour coming, an hour going, and not much to see anyway—just some old bangles being cut out of plastic." He quickly adds, "But maybe I can salvage a couple of shots if the wedding turns out to be nice."

IN THE EVENING, Bill and I go over to Mahesh's and Nimi's to check on the lighting arrangements for the wedding the next day. It is the third evening of the singsong, and, to my amazement, the bridegroom, Anil, is here, in defiance of tradition, which bars the bridegroom from seeing the bride for days before the wedding.

"How are you coming to the wedding?" I ask him, over the singing and the mesmerizing drumbeat.

"We're going to drive over here from our house, and then I'm going to walk up the driveway," he says.

"Can you ride up to the house on a horse?" Bill

asks, joining us. "Isn't that what the bridegroom would generally do? It would make a nice picture."

"I'd be delighted to ride on a horse if we can make the necessary arrangements," Anil says. "My hobby is flying gliders. Would you like to take a photograph of that sometime?"

"No, no. The horse will do," Bill says.

February 23rd

"I WAS UP TILL TWO TRYING TO GET THROUGH TO my wife in London," Ivan says at breakfast in the coffee shop.

"I was up all night trying to get through to Araminta," Bill says. "Bloody Indian telephones. They look like the real thing until you pick one up and try to get hold of someone."

"Bill, remember that job offer I told you about?" Ivan asks. "It begins on the eleventh of March. I've turned it down, so that you can have your full pound of flesh."

"At this rate, I'll need everybody for the full four weeks of shooting," Bill says.

"Do you ever worry that as a free-lancer you might not have enough work?" I ask Ivan.

"Never," he says. "There's always too much work. In fact, I hate to work. I would like to hurt myself—just a little—so that I could collect insurance, and rest in England. As it is, I hardly ever get to see my wife and children."

"We all dream of collecting insurance and taking a rest," Bill says. "But we'd be bored stiff, wouldn't we?"

"What's the main thing on the agenda today?" Ivan asks. "Wedding and more wedding?"

Everyone laughs.

I leave them at breakfast and drive across to my parents' house to make sure that Chachaji can come to the bangle ceremony this morning.

Chachaji, as part of what he calls the "program" of his day, is having early-morning tea—bed tea—with them. He is sitting with Daddyji and amusing him with stories of the bazaar and of his boss. There is something of the jester in him.

"Are you coming to the bangle ceremony this morning?" I ask Chachaji.

"It is during office hours, and Chopra Sahib would dismiss me," he says.

"But he talked to us so nicely yesterday," I say.

"You don't know the real Chopra Sahib," he says guardedly. "Chopra Sahib has a sweet tongue but a counterfeit heart. His words ring like real silver, but in his heart there is only lead. Maybe if you ask him he'll let me come."

Chachaji likes to play the fool, but he is also cunning. Indeed, I reflect, without a certain amount of cunning he could not have survived in the slippery vortex of the Indian streets.

I get Chopra on the telephone and arrange for Chachaji to have the day off.

We all—family, friends, and film team—gather for the bangle ceremony on the lawn of Mahesh's and Nimi's house, under the morning sun. The officiating

Brahman sits in front of the traditional brazier, with Rajani on his right, and leads everyone in the recitation of mantras. Chachaji sits close to them and recites the mantras with great fervor, his dissonant, nasal voice as distinct as the Brahman's powerful, deep one. At a cue from the Brahman, I struggle to get the twelve bangles onto Rajani's wrists. They are a snug fit, and although they have been soaked in milk to make them slide on easily, it still takes me some time. The Brahman invokes the blessings of the gods and leads us in prayer.

Ivan works fast, moving from one end of the gathering to the other so quickly that he sometimes seems to be in two places at once.

After the ceremony, friends and family mill about on the lawn and chat, but Chachaji makes straight for a buffet table that has been set up at one end of the lawn. He piles his plate with as much food as it will hold, and stations himself right next to the table, keeping his eyes on the food; he seems to be already calculating his chances for seconds.

As others start going up to the buffet table for their food, they greet him. "Food up to your standards, Chachaji?"

"Hmm. Very tasty," Chachaji replies laconically, concentrating on his plate.

Around noon, we leave the family and drive to the Bhogal Bazaar area again to have Chachaji show us the buses he often takes to go on his errands. He is confused and anxious. He doesn't understand why he has to take a bus when we have the cars and Chopra Sahib has not given him an errand—a "mission," as he calls it. I try to explain to him that Bill wants him to pretend he is going on a mission, so that we can film him. He doesn't seem to grasp either the idea of make-believe or the idea of a moving picture. But he does what I ask. He joins the crowd at a bus stand and tells people proudly, "A photograph is being taken." He seems to have decided that we are compiling snapshots for a family album, a little book held together with a silk cord.

As always, the camera attracts a huge crowd, and, no matter what I say, people won't stop staring into it.

"This is hopeless!" Bill says. "How can we get a shot of Chacha getting on a bus with this mob all around us?"

Suddenly, the bus arrives, at great speed. Jane claps the board, and Ivan starts shooting. Everyone is shoving to get on the bus. It's a wonder Chachaji isn't pushed to the ground and trampled on. The bus stops for only a few seconds, and then pulls away. Scores of people run after it and crowd their way inside—the bus has no doors at the entrance. A few of them catch hold of the window rails or the entrance rails and hang perilously from the outside as the bus gathers speed. Chachaji is left behind, with a lot of other people. He looks wistfully after the bus. Ivan dashes up an embankment to get away from the crowd and take some shots from above.

Another bus draws up. Chachaji runs to get on but absentmindedly goes past the entrance. By the time he realizes his mistake and turns back, the bus is pulling away.

Bill tells Chachaji to be sure to catch the next bus.

Chachaji starts running, although there isn't a bus in sight. We call him back.

"That last shot's no good!" Ivan shouts, scrambling down the embankment. "I cut it."

"God damn," Bill says, under his breath, and then, encouragingly, to Ivan, "Never mind. I can make a whole sequence of Chacha missing buses."

Ivan crosses the road and starts shooting Chachaji waiting for a bus from there. The crowd, eager to help Chachaji get his picture taken, pushes him up front, so that he is starting the queue instead of bringing up the rear.

Bill is in despair. "In that high shot, Chacha was being shoved by eighty or a hundred people, and now he looks like the leader of the crowd. How will I ever cut the two shots into the same sequence?"

I harangue the crowd, telling them that they are spoiling the picture and shouldn't interfere. I give Chachaji specific directions for taking the next bus.

No matter how often we ask him to take a bus, he tries to do it, mechanically, without a protest—as if to take a bus were just one more order from a superior—but always in vain. He doesn't once ask how he performed or how the picture came out. When he is asked to do something all over again, he simply says, "Never mind. Let it be." Moreover, unlike the people crowding around, who cannot take their eyes off the camera, Chachaji never so much as glances at it.

Bill tells Ivan to get on the next bus with Chachaji and do some tracking shots. The rest of us get into the cars and prepare to follow the bus.

A bus arrives and pulls out, and we chase it. Then

Yoginder Singh cries out, "Sahib, there's Chacha! He seems to be walking home!"

"Oh, my God!" Bill shouts. "Ivan must have got on the bus by himself!" Yoginder Singh jumps out of the car, grabs Chachaji, and virtually throws him into the back of the car, and we race after the bus. The bus rushes along past several bus stands, and it begins to seem as though it would never stop.

Eventually, we get a shot of Chachaji boarding the bus with Ivan, but nowhere near the bus stand he would normally use to do an errand from the Pharmacy of Prosperity. We also get tracking shots of Chachaji sitting in the bus and looking out, of Chachaji moving through the bus, of Chachaji getting off the bus.

Suddenly, Chachaji says to me in his thin little voice, "Enough."

It's two-thirty, and everyone is worn out and wants to stop for lunch.

"Tell the old sod he can now eat himself sick with *samosas* on Cran Productions' expense account," Bill says, with a laugh.

Jane and Sally, after conferring, announce that they both thought that at the crucial moment—when Chachaji was getting on the bus with Ivan—Chachaji had looked at the camera.

"Damn!" Bill exclaims. "But I'm not about to retrace my steps and go through that whole bus business again. I'll simply have to fudge it in the cutting room. Our shots of buses rushing across the film will create a certain confusion, and then no one will notice whether he looked at the camera or not. They'll just remember what he had to go through to deliver one crummy little bottle."

❧

ALL AFTERNOON, Bill has been talking about "the dreaded arrival." It seems that Araminta is joining us. She has got some sort of assignment to do research in Delhi for an article, and has decided to combine it with a holiday here.

"That's excellent," Ivan says. "Now we'll have three women. Location work shouldn't be for men only."

"Women always change things," Bill says.

❧

AT SIX O'CLOCK, outside Mahesh's and Nimi's house, Ivan balances himself on a balustrade with a clear view of the driveway, which is about a hundred yards long, waiting for the bridegroom to arrive on his horse, in the company of his relatives. Colored lights are strung around the house and garden, making a very festive scene in the dusk. The bridegroom's party arrives in a rush, with a brass band playing Indian film tunes.

I move forward with Rajani's other male relatives for the traditional greeting ceremony. Bill has told Ivan to film us embracing our opposite numbers in the bridegroom's party. There is a great din of people

trying to find their opposite numbers to embrace cere-
monially. Several people embrace me, probably confusing me with some other uncle or brother.

Above the turmoil, I hear Bill shouting, "Can't
someone keep these hordes back? They're ruining the
shot!" There are so many people in the driveway that
the bridegroom can make little headway on his horse.
Bill, furious, elbows his way over to me through the
melee. "God!" he mutters through his teeth. "At this
rate, it'll take him twenty minutes to get up the driveway. And then all those people! You couldn't tell who
was who—which were his relatives, which were hers."

"This is a documentary, Bill, and that's how weddings go," I say. "The bridegroom did agree to arrive
on a horse just for the camera."

We both laugh.

There is a sudden commotion where the crowd is
thickest. Everyone runs to see what has happened. One
of Ivan's lights, which was hung from a tree, has fallen
down. "If this had been ten years ago, there would
have been an explosion and people hurt," Bill says.
"My God! The whole branch came down. You can't
even depend on the trees here."

Later, everyone relaxes over dinner on the lawn.
Jane has abandoned her jeans for the occasion and
looks very pretty in a long evening dress, with a jade
ring on one finger and a locket around her neck.

After the religious ceremony, we all follow the
young couple as they head for the bridegroom's car, to
the sad parting tune of high-pitched Indian bagpipes.
Everyone is suddenly silent, and many people are tear-
ful. This moment marks the symbolic passing away of

the young girl. (She will be reborn when she reaches her new home, and there will be renewed rejoicing.)

"How did the shooting go?" I ask Bill. I have had to stick with the family much of the time, and have not been able to follow the shooting closely.

"I think we got some nice impressionistic shots of the lights," Bill says. "They make the whole place look like a fairyland. I think we got another really nice shot of Chacha eating. We also got a good shot of the actual ceremony. The bride and groom looked really sweet. I think we got a very nice shot of everyone throwing flower petals at the bride and groom. Chacha looked really sweet, too, throwing his little handful of flowers."

February 24th

BILL HAS CALLED FOR THE CARS AND THE CREW TO be here at nine. The cars are here but the crew isn't. He looks at his watch and, exactly at nine, walks over to the Ambassador, gets in, slams the door hard, and curses. He drums on the dashboard. Then he jokes with Sally, as if he were unconcerned, but his anger still shows in his eyes. Whatever time he calls the crew for, somebody is always slightly late. Each time, he gets angry, and each time, after giving vent to his anger, he jokes. Today, as usual, Ivan, Eoin, and Jane straggle out and breezily pretend not to notice Bill's anger.

We drive to the Pharmacy of Prosperity, where we want to build up Chachaji's working day—his program—and develop some sequences showing his relationship with his employers.

"I want to get more of the squalor on film," Bill says. "I want to sneak a shot of the wretched bottle washer—maybe with Chacha looking on."

We start speculating, as we have done more than once, on the nature of Chopra's business. He seems to have no customers, no merchandise for sale which we've been able to discover, no incoming deliveries—no traffic of any kind. He seems to have no permanent staff. In fact, Chachaji seems to be his only full-time employee, and even he is kept on simply from day to day. It's hard to understand why they employ a slow, eighty-three-year-old man to run errands when they could easily hire some quick young fellow for just a little more money. And why should Chopra be doing business out of such a dilapidated old house, filled with what looks like rubbish?

"I think that Pharmacy of Prosperity, or whatever the dump is called, is a front for something," Bill says. "Chacha is kept around because he provides a good cover. Maybe the film can be an exposé."

When we pull up at the Pharmacy of Prosperity, Chopra, who has been standing in the little courtyard, scowls and strides into his shop, slamming the screen door and banging the inside doors shut.

"What do you suppose is the matter with him?" Bill asks.

"I think he thinks we are being nosy," I say. "For all I know, he thinks we are government agents, snooping around to catch him out in some violation or other. People here tend to be very suspicious."

"What do we do now?" Bill asks, settling back in his seat and drumming on the dashboard.

"We can't afford to antagonize him, or we may not be able to film Chachaji working here at all," I say. "I was surprised that he coöperated with us in the first place. Maybe he was taken by the novelty of the idea. But now he's had time for second thoughts."

"May I say something, Ved Sahib?" Yoginder Singh asks, in Punjabi. "I think Chopra Sahib wants some consideration. He sees these white sahibs and this expensive equipment. He knows about Hollywood. If you give me permission, I will go inside and have a frank talk with him."

I interpret for Bill, and explain to him that "frank talk" is a euphemism for a bribe, which is usually negotiated through an intermediary, to save face all around.

"There is no provision in the budget for bribes," Bill objects. Then he says impetuously, "Hell, send Yoginder Singh in and start negotiations."

I veto the idea, on practical as well as moral grounds. A bribe could jeopardize not only the film but also Chachaji's livelihood. I suggest a bold approach—that we all simply go in as if nothing had changed.

When we enter the store, Chopra is typing away furiously and young Chopra is on the telephone. They both ignore us. When young Chopra puts the telephone down, he asks me, with a touch of exasperation, "Why are you doing a film on Bahali Ram? Whom is it for?"

I tell him that through Bahali Ram we hope to

tell the story of one man's survival in India, and that we have tentatively chosen him because he is my relative. I emphasize that the film is for educational television.

"You have so many relatives—why Bahali Ram?" young Chopra asks. "He's a very bad advertisement for the motherland."

I explain to him that we are interested not in advertising India but in depicting life as it is lived here.

He keeps on making the same point, using such phrases as "Show some nice-looking people," "Show our spiritual heritage," "Don't expose our poverty," and "Don't expose our weakness."

Finally, Chopra, who has kept right on typing, looks up and says, "How can we have any objection? Bahali Ram is a free man, and you can film him any time. But you are disrupting our business. We have to earn our bread, too. Anyway, he is gone for the day."

"Where did he go?"

"We gave him a check to cash at the bank in Bhogal Bazaar," young Chopra says. "But he is a man of his own moods. You can never be sure when he'll do a job or how long he will take doing it."

"Ask him if I can take a shot or two of the shop," Ivan whispers to me.

But before I can do so, Chopra says sternly, "There is nothing to see here. Please do not bother us any further."

We leave quickly and go to Bhogal Bazaar in search of Chachaji.

As we pull up in front of the bank, Yoginder

Singh collapses into laughter, his whole body shaking. "There has never been a cavalcade like this before, looking for a poor peon."

Bill and I find Chachaji inside the bank, sitting on a bench, patiently waiting to be called. Left to himself, he would probably be kept waiting for a few more hours, but because of our presence he is able to get the check cashed quickly. This time, despite the omnipresent ogling crowd, we succeed in taking a couple of shots of him walking through the bazaar, and then Ivan goes off on his own to take cut-away shots: people shaving on the street; people squatting in the hope of some odd job; people hawking; people barrelling along on bicycles. He rejoins us in a few minutes.

As we drive Chachaji back to the Pharmacy of Prosperity, I say to him, "Find out what errands they want you to do today, and we'll take you there and film you doing them."

"Let it be," Chachaji says. "These people at banks and such are not sympathetic. They should not have their photographs taken for abroad. If you want more photographs of me, you can take them just now, here in the motorcar."

"But we want to show how you spend your day," I say.

"Whatever you say," Chachaji says.

We wait in the cars a little distance from the Pharmacy of Prosperity while Chachaji goes in. He returns with two strenuous errands to do. One of them is to deposit a check at the State Bank, in Old Delhi, many miles away. That errand alone would take him a whole day if he were to go his usual way—in buses, in bicycle rickshaws, and on foot. The other is to pick up some forms at the tax office in New Delhi; the office is closer than the bank, but this errand could involve long waits and several visits, over several days.

"Chopra Sahib wants to keep Chachaji busy and out of our reach," Yoginder Singh says. "He can't imagine that Chachaji is suddenly so important that the Sahibs will drive him on his errands."

It takes us more than an hour to weave our way to Old Delhi through the lunchtime traffic.

The bank has an impressive, almost majestic façade. As we are about to take a shot of Chachaji going in, security guards materialize and try to confiscate our equipment. I ask to see the manager, and eventually Bill and I are shown into his office. The manager is on the telephone, getting advice—apparently from an astrologer—about his six-year-old son, who is running a high fever.

When the manager hangs up, I explain our purpose.

"No one is allowed to take a picture of a government building without proper permissions from higher-ups," he says distractedly. "But I'll make an exception if you do it quickly."

The bank is thronged, and the crowds are unruly. They look at the camera, shout directions to Chachaji, and generally get in the way. The bank officials drop their work and come over to stare. Ivan somehow remains calm under pressure, and is able to get shots of Chachaji walking up to the counter and talking to a teller.

"This check isn't endorsed," the teller says. "You

Chachaji in Delhi

must first go to another bank, in New Delhi, for proper endorsement, and then come back here."

"Isn't endorsed?" Chachaji says, not incredulously—that might give offense—but, rather, like an old man who is a little hard of hearing, as indeed he is. He quickly adds, "Never mind. I will go there some other day and then come back."

"That bank sequence was rotten," Bill says when we are back in the Ambassador. "Too many bloody people getting in the way, and the shots were disconnected. We might as well have stayed in bed this morning. I still think Chacha's a mistake. There's not much action in his life, and what little there is can't really be filmed."

I try to cheer him up. "Indian banks are very confusing places. It may look better than you think. And maybe we'll have better luck in the tax office. It's a much smaller place and should be easier to control."

The tax office is up a dirty stairway and off a long veranda covered with bird droppings. It is a small, dingy room with many desks, many typewriters, and innumerable file folders stuffed with papers and tied with red tapes.

Bill rallies. "This is ideal! It's just right for Chacha."

Chachaji asks for the forms, and the clerk says that he has come on the wrong day—forms are given out only on Saturdays. It is a telling exchange, showing the bureaucratic pettifogging that Chachaji has to suffer every day.

We decide to use the rest of the day to work on Chachaji's morning routine, even though it is getting to be evening, for the morning and evening light are similar. Ivan sets up the camera in Chachaji's little room, and we film him going through his precise, cramped motions: getting up; covering his head with a muffler; slipping into his sandals; shuffling across to the lavatory and going into the adjacent washroom.

At one point, Bill decides that Chachaji has muffed his walk by hesitating on his way to the lavatory. He slips into Chachaji's squeaky sandals and walks the stretch himself. Eoin is suddenly galvanized into action and follows, catlike, with his microphone, to record the sound of Bill's walk. Bill mimics the walk so well, reproduces the characteristic sounds so accurately—the tentative, gingerly footfalls, the squeaks and shuffles, the clickings and flappings—that, hearing him, one would never imagine that anyone but Chachaji was walking. Meanwhile, Chachaji sits on his bed with his usual deadpan expression, as if he didn't have the faintest idea what Bill is up to, and didn't care.

"Yeah," Bill says, pleased with himself. "I'll be able to repeat that sound and drop it anywhere I like in the house sequences."

"Yeah—how come no one ever remembers the sound man?" Eoin says, a bit caustically, and he goes on, "People remember directors, maybe cameramen, but do you know anyone who can name a single sound man?"

I will certainly remember Eoin McCann: how, when he is not recording, he stands watching the shooting, his hands folded in front of him, rather like a minister outside a church waiting to greet the members of his congregation; how he seems almost to hear with his eyes; how he nods appreciatively after an especially good shot.

We now set up the camera in the doorway of the kitchen, off the back veranda, to film Chachaji making his tea. He bends in front of an open fire, which he keeps alive by blowing on it in short puffs; boils some water and tea leaves together in a cheap-looking pot; pours the tea through a strainer into a mug, rattling the two against each other as he does so; slowly transfers the tea from the mug into a cup, to cool it.

"My God! We can't show all that," Bill says. "It's too tedious. I know, I'll cut out the cup and make him seem to drink out of the mug. Then the tea sequence should work fine."

"Did you get all the sounds, Eoin?" I ask.

"I think so," he says, and he adds thoughtfully, "A good sound man is not committed to getting literally every last gurgle. He has to use his imagination, project what the film will end up being, and capture the most appropriate sounds for it."

We go with Chachaji to his son Madan's, a short distance away on the other side of some railway tracks, where he usually has his evening meal. Madan, who works as a clerk of a clerk of a small-time transport company, lives with his wife, Vimla, and their two children—a boy of eighteen and a girl of thirteen—in a couple of rooms in a tenement. The whole family are as respectful of Chachaji as Chachaji is of Daddyji. We set up the camera in the doorway of the main room and film the family at their meal. They eat in eerie silence, as if every morsel of food must be savored without the distraction of talk. In the background, there are the sounds of trains shunting and clattering. There is something mournful and touching about the little family huddled together against the world.

I can tell that Bill is much taken with the scene, because he is more than usually agitated about the camerawork. "That was lovely, but are you sure the camera was focussed? It didn't look steady to me," he says to Ivan.

Ivan laughs and reassures him. He seems to be getting used to Bill's anxieties, and anyway he is not the kind of man to get ruffled.

"It's a 'Last Supper' scene," Bill says contentedly.

February 25th

B ILL HAS CALLED THE CREW FOR 6:15 A.M., AND, for once, Jane comes down early. She starts to walk briskly toward the cars, then stops. Yoginder Singh is sitting behind the steering wheel of the Ambassador without his turban, completely absorbed in combing out his hair, which hangs down to his hips and is shiny with oil. Now and again, he pauses to pinch lice off his scalp and kill them with a flick of the fingernail. Jane hesitates and half turns back. Yoginder Singh catches sight of her and bursts out laughing. He beckons to her not to leave, and quickly bundles up his hair and dons his turban.

We arrive at Chachaji's house a little after six-

thirty. Chachaji has already left to collect his daily government ration of milk from a kiosk a few hundred
yards away. We hurry after him and arrive at the kiosk
just as he is reaching the head of the milk queue.

"It's great," Bill says, looking at Chachaji's pink
turban in the hazy early-morning light. He runs up to
Chachaji and stops him from getting the milk until
Ivan can set up a shot. We film Chachaji returning two
empty milk bottles, receiving two full ones, and starting home. He is so preoccupied with getting the milk
home that he goes off without us.

Back at the house, Chachaji says, "Arya Samaj people are expected any minute. If I don't have the front
veranda ready for them promptly, they will eat a lot
of anger and then vent it on me."

Chachaji sets about his tasks before the camera,
and Yoginder Singh and Amarjit Singh waylay a few
elderly worshippers straggling in for their morning
prayers. To the amusement of the whole team, Chachaji performs his duties in a very perfunctory way,
apparently considering them beneath his station. He
sweeps the front veranda absently without disturbing
the dust. He goes through the motions of shaking out
the prayer mat without really shaking it, and sets out
the prayer implements—a brazier for the sacred fire,
firewood, bowls of incense and ghi, fire tongs—any
which way. The congregation moves onto the veranda,
and Chachaji is about to join it for the prayers, but Bill
intercepts him and has him stand and watch, with the
idea of making him look like a solitary old man, an
outsider.

After the take, Chachaji wants to go. "I am late with the milk for Madan's tea," he says. "The photographs are delaying my program. Madan will have to go to work without his tea and he will eat anger."

Bill suggests that we take him and his milk to Madan's in the car, and film scenes on the way to show Chachaji's daily route. Chachaji complains that he will be late, but sets about putting the two bottles of milk on the floor of the Ambassador. As he is getting in, he almost knocks one over, and some milk splashes onto the floor. He is distraught over the loss.

From the front seat, Yoginder Singh good-humoredly scolds Chachaji. "You're stinking up my car!" he says. "It will make a bad impression on the white sahibs and memsahibs."

Chachaji replies, "There is no need for the milk to be driven. I should have carried it, as always. I'm getting late. There should be enough photographs by now."

"What's he saying? What's he saying?" Bill asks me. "Tell him we need many more photographs for his American admirers."

It's hot, and the smell of the spilt milk does fill the car. Bill ostentatiously holds his nose.

We have to cross the four-hundred-year-old Twelve Column Bridge, which now spans one of the city's main sullage drains, to get to Madan's house.

"This will make a wonderful shot—the passage of time amidst squalor," Bill says.

Bill has Ivan set up the camera in the middle of the bridge, so that he can include in his shot an old monument, the sullage drain, and some poor people. I tell Chachaji to walk across the bridge and pass the camera, keeping to the left side.

"Cran Sahib, please get this photograph quickly," Chachaji says. "Madan has gone to work without his tea. My daughter-in-law is waiting for me to eat breakfast. I am late for Chopra Sahib."

At first, Chachaji may have been flattered by all the attention we were paying him, even if he was somewhat wary of it, but now he is apparently starting to view us as an unwelcome intrusion in his daily routine.

Bill is alternately exasperated and amused that something as insignificant as delivering milk should interfere with the expensive process of filming. "Just two minutes more, Chacha," he says. "Just two minutes more of your valuable time."

Bill signals to Ivan to start shooting, and shoves Chachaji in the direction of the camera. Then he turns to me and says, "I bet you ten rupees the old sod will end up on the right side of the damn bridge." Even as he is talking—a little disdainfully, rather like a British commanding officer at the high noon of the raj—Chachaji starts veering to the right.

Jane runs up to him and sets him straight.

"Interference. Interference. I withdraw my bet," Bill says.

We come to the railway tracks, and Ivan sets up the camera on some high ground, near a signalman's hut, where goats and cows are grazing. Bill loves the look of Indian trains, which are often bright-colored and as crowded as the bazaars, and he is eager to have a shot of Chachaji dwarfed by a train in the background.

I ask the signalman the time of the next train.

"In about ten minutes," he says, and, to our surprise, he adds, "But I don't know which direction it will come from."

Bill posts Chachaji beside the tracks with Sally nearby, so that if the train comes from the opposite direction she can quickly take him to the right spot.

We wait and watch—ten, twenty, twenty-five minutes—without a sign of a train. Chachaji gets more restive by the minute, but Bill jollies him along. Finally, a train comes into view, and, as luck would have it, Chachaji is in the right spot.

The camera rolls to pick up the train in the distance. But Chachaji is so eager to get the ordeal over with that he starts walking before the train has caught up with him, even though we all yell at him to go back and wait until the train comes abreast of him. Either he doesn't hear or he doesn't understand, and we get a shot that looks as if he were racing the train—and winning.

"Jesus!" Bill exclaims. "If I were to tell my friends at the BBC that we wasted half an hour of good shooting time for a bloody shot of a train—and a bad one, at that—they would laugh me out of the business."

At Madan's, we film Chachaji eating his breakfast, with the sound of an engine hissing in the background. Chachaji's daughter-in-law asks him repeatedly why he is so late, but he is uncommunicative and concentrates on his food.

Bill is happy with the breakfast shot. "Well, we're building up his morning, all right," he says. "I just wish the bloody routine had more action in it."

As soon as Chachaji has finished his breakfast, we

rush him to the Pharmacy of Prosperity and then go over to my parents' house for our own breakfast.

Kate, a friend of my sister Usha's from Kalamazoo who has been staying in my parents' house, takes a cup of coffee out to Yoginder Singh. He has drawn up a chair in the shade on the veranda, and is sitting there like an old family retainer. He once worked for Mahesh and knows all the members of the family—what their relationships are, even how they feel about each other. Amarjit Singh is standing stiffly by the station wagon and watching Yoginder Singh disapprovingly, as if Yoginder Singh were an overgrown kid taking liberties unworthy of a good servant. Kate, however, now takes Amarjit Singh a cup of coffee, too. He is flabbergasted and shrinks from it. She presses it on him, and her natural friendliness eventually wins him over. He takes the coffee, and is effusive in his thanks, then quickly reverts to his old, sombre self.

At lunch at the Imperial, Bill sounds a little more enthusiastic about the Chacha film. His mood keeps changing, and, whether he knows it or not, the rapid changes have the effect of prodding me into thinking up new material for filming. Ivan, Eoin, and Jane still seem to me to be cool to the idea of the Chacha film, though they are careful never to volunteer their opinions. I ask myself if their lack of enthusiasm isn't to be expected, since they work on the film only in bits and pieces, and our film, even more than most, will be made or unmade in the editing—a process in which they, of course, will have no part. Still, I try to draw them out.

"Who says we're against the film?" Ivan says flippantly. He has trouble being serious about anything for very long. "We have no opinions. We just do what we're told. It's your film and Bill's."

I press him.

"The film seems to be all in the same tone—with no relief," he says seriously, and he adds, "I like action and drama in a film—guns and molls."

"Have you seen any of Satyajit Ray's films?" I ask. "I want the Chacha film to have something of their feeling and tone."

" 'Pather Panchali' has to be one of the most boring films I've ever seen," he says.

"That's not what he really thinks," Jane says. "He sat through the whole trilogy, all shown at one time."

"But Satyajit Ray is short on laughs," Bill puts in. "My idea of a good film is a joke a minute."

Back at our hotel, a shipping agent, a well-spoken young man, meets Bill and me in the coffee shop, by appointment. We have a cup of tea, and Bill gives him all the rolls of film and the tapes we have used so far, along with completed customs-declaration forms and the appropriate shooting-log cards, for immediate dispatch to the States. Bill tells me that in a matter of a few days the film will be developed and the sound synchronized, and David Fanning and the production manager of "World," Christopher Gilbert, will screen the rushes and send us their reactions.

After the shipping agent leaves, Bill sends a cable

to "GHQ"—his term for the television station—saying, "DUE AIRPORT AND CURRENCY COMPLICATIONS AM ADVISED BEST TO SHIP FILM ON COLLECT PAYMENT BASIS STOP WGBH CAN DEBIT CRAN PRODUCTIONS LATER STOP CANST CONFIRM QUESTION GRATEFUL YOU RING MY WIFE."

Back at the tea table, Bill announces to me, "Almost five days of shooting, and I'll wager we haven't got even three minutes of usable film. That's about three-quarters of a minute per day."

He has made a list of the sequences we have shot, with the time he estimates each will "play" once it is edited down. He claims that the State Bank sequence, which took us almost half a day to get "in the can," won't play for more than twenty seconds—or maybe not at all, since he thinks that no one will be able to make out what's happening, with all the crowds and confusion. The tax-office sequence, he claims, is worth only fifteen seconds, and most of that, too, may have to be discarded, because it looks "too ordinary and drab." All the morning-routine sequences, he claims, add up to about a minute, which is as long as Bill thinks they can hold the interest of the viewers. And so on.

I challenge his estimates, contending that the morning sequences alone could be worth five minutes, because they have a certain lyrical quality. But Bill is adamant. He rubs in the fact that he is a professional filmmaker and I am not. He once again questions the whole idea of a film about Chachaji for a documentary on India.

"I still think our best hope is to make a slow, intense film about Chachaji," I say.

"It'll be slow, all right," Bill says glumly. "But, even so, I can't see us dragging it on for fifty-seven minutes. That's the exact time that I have to fill on the air—not a minute more or less. And, remember, we have to hold the interest of anywhere up to *twen-ty mil-lion* people. I think we have squeezed Chacha dry. There may still be an odd sequence or two to fill out his day, but I don't see that we can do a hell of a lot more with him." He carelessly spreads some jam on a piece of toast. "A film about India has to be about villagers—all those poor people. Your family is too Westernized. And every goddam one of them lives in the city." Bill constantly veers between the journalist out to do a newsworthy film portraying "the abyss of Indian poverty," as he calls it, and the artist who doesn't want to miss an opportunity to do an original film, which might "get a prize."

Ivan joins us. "Delhi has boring architecture," he says, pouring himself some tea. "You could say that it's not exactly a cameraman's dream."

"Delhi just looks too Western for a film about India," Bill agrees. Then, to me, he says, "The crew are itching to travel. They would like to see something of real India, even if it is just the countryside near Delhi. Can we go somewhere tomorrow? And the crew think boring old Chacha and boring old Delhi might not make the most exciting film."

"We could go to Hardwar," I say. "It's a few hours' drive. It's an ancient Hindu place of pilgrimage on the Ganges. The Ganges—or Ganga, in Hindi—has probably played a greater part in Indian history and mythology than any river has played in the life of any other country. I know Chachaji would like to make the pilgrimage to Hardwar before he dies."

"The holy men and all those pilgrims would make wonderful shots," Bill says, warming to the idea and puffing vigorously at his pipe.

We decide to leave for Hardwar the next day around noon and spend the night there, provided I can make the necessary arrangements.

As we are going upstairs to our rooms, Bill says, "To be frank, I have been to-ing and fro-ing in my mind about taking Chacha with us. I have just about had it with Chacha. It's the same thing over and over. As you heard for yourself, the crew agree with me. Besides, there won't be room for him in the cars. We should take your parents. They are strong characters. We should really develop them and try to make a family film."

I try to argue that we should also take Chachaji with us, but again Bill is adamant. I give in, murmuring, "It's a director's film, after all."

I run into Sally and tell her that we are going to Hardwar but are not taking Chachaji with us.

"Why not?" she asks.

"It seems Bill has given up the idea of a film about Chachaji for one about the whole family."

"Don't you let him do it!" Sally says.

"It's a director's film," I repeat lamely.

"But it's your film, too," she says. "You shouldn't give up the Chacha idea without a fight."

"You're right."

Encouraged by Sally, I go up to Bill's room.

"What the hell!" Bill says, suddenly agreeable.

"We owe him a good bath in the Ganges. Meanwhile, let's do the epiphany scene—Chacha appearing for dinner with your family."

❧

For Chachaji, the most propitious time to drop in on his well-off relatives is mealtime. He particularly likes dropping in when he spots a couple of familiar cars outside the house, since they are an omen of a family gathering; or when he spies a servant returning from the bazaar with some delicacies, since that is an omen of a happy occasion. As a poor relation, he has certain unstated rights—at least in the house of God-fearing relations—and he knows how to exercise them. He times his arrival carefully, being aware that if he arrives too early he may be sent off with just some appetizers and if he arrives too late there may not be a chance for seconds, while if he arrives on the dot his relatives will have no choice but to include him, and there will be no danger of his being shortchanged.

I worry a bit about the strain on my parents of filming a family meal in their house. Daddyji has been a heart patient for the last twelve years, and one of Mamaji's two house servants is sick. But my sisters Nimi and Umi say they will organize a pool of servants and dishes—something they do practically every week anyway, for family gatherings. In any case, they assure me, Daddyji's involvement in the film is good for him.

I coach Chachaji for his part in the scene and station him on the front veranda. Nimi, Umi, and Usha, with their husbands and children, take their places at the table—on a closed-in back veranda, next to the kitchen, that serves as a dining room. Usha's husband, an American, known to one and all as Art, quietly sits down next to Usha, and she starts serving him.

As Jane is about to put up the board, Bill comes up to me and whispers, "Jesus Christ, we can't have Art in the picture. He sticks out like a sore thumb. You have to get him out."

I agree that Art, who is big and tall and fair-skinned, stands out as a very American presence in an Indian family setting, but I say that an American son-in-law is a mark of the family's cosmopolitanism.

"You can't start putting such nuances in," Bill says. "Art simply looks too incongruous in a film about India."

I take Usha to one side and explain the problem to her.

"But I think Art wants to be in the film," she says. "I think he's looking forward to having his parents in the States see him sitting with us at the table as one of our family. He'll be hurt."

"I understand the way he feels. But will you talk to him?"

She does, and Art gives us a hurt look, gets up, and leaves.

Usha also starts to leave. "I don't want to be in the film, either," she whispers to me. "Art is part of me."

Daddyji, made uncomfortable by the presence of the camera, is getting agitated and wants to know what's going on. The atmosphere has become tense. I prevail upon Usha to take a seat. Bill quickly removes Art's chair and place setting, rearranges the chairs, and calls for the board. I hurriedly find my place at the table, too. (I have become part of the film again, as at the bangle cutter's and at the bangle ceremony.)

We start eating, trying hard to be ourselves. As we talk, we relax a little, and even find it amusing that such a routine occurrence is being staged for the camera. Eoin stands in one corner, watching, and a slow, appreciative smile comes over his face.

On cue, Yoginder Singh propels Chachaji into our midst. Umi, following instructions that Bill gave earlier, gets up and places a chair—the lowest we have—on Daddyji's right for Chachaji, who sits down in it. (As a rule, Chachaji would sit in an ordinary chair anywhere he could find a place at the table.) The chair is so low and Chachaji so small that his chin almost touches the tabletop. As Umi starts piling food on the plate set in front of him, he looks a bit like a mouse in a cartoon who has been invited to a giant's feast. (The scene may be correct in symbolically depicting Chachaji's position in the family and, by analogy, in the world, but, as Daddyji later points out repeatedly, "it is not the way we treat Bahali Ram every day.")

Daddyji is eager that every member of the family appear at his or her best in the film, and be seen as respectful to Chachaji. Daddyji received part of his education in the West, and there has been hardly a year in the last twenty-five when he has not spent some time there; he is aware, in a way that the others are not, of the power of television and of how the camera can distort. He knows that the film will expose an intimate family moment to public scrutiny, and he does not wish us to make a spectacle of ourselves. But Mahesh, who is very photogenic, seems excited by the thought of being in a film that will be seen on television by his airline associates in the States, and plays to the camera without much concern about the impression he will make on people who don't know him. He teases Chachaji, and that has the effect of drawing Chachaji out. Chachaji tells some tangled jokes in Punjabi, and there is general, if somewhat self-conscious, laughter. Everyone seems slightly on edge—everyone except Chachaji. This is the first time we have been able to film him talking and laughing, and having the family's real attention. Up to now, we have filmed him only as a kind of sombre automaton directed hither and thither to perform ritualistic feats for the camera.

"That was great," Bill says to me at the end of the take. "I had the idea that Chacha was a solitary old codger, hanging on to his routine like a condemned man. But here we see him really animated, and the contrast is terrific. It adds to his growing mystique. Actually, both the wedding and the dinner scene work well. Maybe I can cut them together to give the impression that the wedding was sort of an early-evening thing and then people came to this dinner."

"No, that won't work," I say. "After the marriage feast, no one would go home and sit down to another meal."

"Damn."

February 26th

O VER EARLY-MORNING COFFEE IN THE COFFEE SHOP, in the middle of talking about the weather, hotel coffee, and hotel insect life, Bill lets drop the fact that Araminta—"the dreaded arrival"— turned up in the middle of the night.

Soon Araminta joins us, and, perhaps sensing that her introduction into what is now a little family could be jarring, she nervously launches into a long story about the tribulations of flying. She has apparently spent three days in airports and on airplanes, because her travel agent booked her on nonexistent flights. "I haven't slept a wink in three days," she says.

"It's the first time I've been on a film unit with so many women," Ivan says gallantly. "They really add a lot."

"I'm not on your film unit," Araminta says. "I'm here to do an article on Canadian-Indian relations for the *Financial Post.*" But when she hears about our plan to go to Hardwar, she announces, "I'm coming with you. I've always wanted to see Hardwar. Bill, you must find a place for me in the car."

"What shooting can we get in this morning, before we leave for Hardwar?" Bill asks.

"Maybe we could do Chacha shaving," I say.

"How, exactly, did Chacha get interested in shaving?" Bill asks. "Wouldn't it have been easier for him just to have a beard?"

"He acquired the habit of shaving as a clerk during the raj, and he has clung to it, as people in a higher station here cling to a coat and tie," I say, and I explain that, in a poor country that has lived under British rule, to be clean-shaven is to have respectability, to be a notch above the natives. Yet most homes have no running water, no table, no chair, no safety razor—above all, no money for blades.

We had previously arranged to meet Chachaji at his house at six-forty-five to do some shooting, and we now rush there to try to "catch him in the act," as Bill puts it. But the front door of Chachaji's room is bolted and padlocked, and there is no sign of him.

"I think he's given us the slip," I say. I have been worried for some time now that the strain of having us all following him around telling him what to do and how and when to do it might be too much for him.

"Oh, God! What do we do now!" Bill asks glumly.

"He couldn't have gone very far," I say, and I take everyone across to my parents' house, next door.

Daddyji, who has characteristically become deeply involved in our project, looks worried. "I don't think Bahali Ram was there all night," he says. "I think he has absconded. He's not dependable for something he doesn't understand. What will you do now? The question is, can you have 'Hamlet' without Hamlet?"

Everyone laughs, relieving the tension.

Mamaji offers us tea, and I go out to the cars and tell Yoginder Singh to go and find Chachaji.

"But where should I look, Ved Sahib?" he asks, starting up the engine.

"Go to the milk kiosk. Go to Madan's. Go to

Bhogal Bazaar. Go to the Pharmacy of Prosperity. Drive around the streets. But find him."

"I'll find him, Sahib, or my name isn't Yoginder Singh!" he says, with a laugh that shakes his huge frame, and the car screeches off.

As I am about to rejoin the others, I hear someone struggling with Chachaji's lock. It is Chachaji himself.

"Where have you been, Chachaji?" I ask.

"Nowhere," he says, without looking up or taking notice that the whole team has trooped across to his house and is now hovering over him. He has his muffler tied around his head, and looks as though he had just waked up. "I was drinking my tea on the back veranda," he says, adding rather querulously, "There wasn't so much as a biscuit to eat with it."

"But why did you lock the door?" Bill asks.

"There are lots of strange parties walking around here these days, and I am responsible for all the Arya Samaj bowls and fire tongs and such." His explanation doesn't sound very plausible, but then I recall that several years ago the Arya Samaj people lost some prayer implements, accused him of stealing them, and threatened to turn him out.

"Chachaji, we'd like to film you shaving," I say.

"Let it be," Chachaji says. "What is there special about shaving? I'm getting late with the milk for Madan's tea. I'm getting late with my program."

I tell him about our plan of taking him to Hardwar, perhaps later that day.

He registers no visible emotion, but says circumspectly, "Going to Hardwar certainly requires a good shave."

Chachaji Early in the Morning

"Tell him the shaving picture won't take long," Bill says. "And ask him where, exactly, he shaves."

"I can shave anywhere I'm sitting," Chachaji says.

"Let him do it on the back veranda, then," Bill says. "The light's better there."

Ivan, Eoin, and Jane get the equipment out of the station wagon.

"Would he sit at that table to shave?" Bill asks, pointing to a table holding a decrepit old harmonium. which the Arya Samajists sometimes use to accompany their hymns. Sally picks out a few notes on the harmonium; they hiss and whine, jangling the nerves.

"I can sit at a table for the photograph if Cran Sahib would like to take a photograph of the table," Chachaji says, suddenly becoming accommodating.

"Does he wear his turban while he shaves?" Bill asks.

Chachaji seems not to grasp what his turban has to do with shaving, but he finally decides that Bill wants his turban in the shaving picture, and says obligingly, "Turban is good for not catching cold."

Bill laughs, and paces up and down looking at the sky. "Dammit! The early-morning light's going, and going fast. We should have been here at six."

Ivan is setting up the camera on a tripod.

"It's nearly seven-thirty," Bill goes on, theatrically looking at his watch. "We are almost an hour into our shooting day and we haven't even set up a shot."

"He'll need a cup or a glass of hot water, Bill," I say.

Bill races off to my parents' house and returns with

a kettle of hot water, but Chachaji has meanwhile heated up his own.

"We just might need some extra hot water," Bill says, laughing. "I've learned not to take chances with old Chacha."

Chachaji sits down at the table with a cup of hot water, a small, napkinlike towel, and an old square tin that once held sweets—a gaudy affair with two luscious women painted on it in blue, green, red, yellow, and orange. Bill moves the table and Chachaji so that the light will fall over Chachaji's shoulder. Jane puts up the board.

From outside come the ubiquitous sounds of crows cawing and of peddlers hawking, the fragments of the peddlers' calls echoing down the street as they walk along or ride past on bicycles: "Washers for leaky taps!" "Puncture repair!" "Bananas! Apples! Oranges!"

Chachaji precisely, methodically opens the tin and takes from it a folding mirror, a shaving brush, a small, flat tin with soap in it, a safety razor, and a razor blade, in its waxed-paper wrapping, which is clearly marked in pencil "22/2/78"—probably the date when he first began using that particular blade.

Bill suddenly tenses: the shaving brush is already wet. "Bloody Chacha! He's shaved already!" he mutters.

Chachaji, oblivious of everything, dips his shaving brush in the cup of water and soaps his face. He shaves with quick, even strokes.

Bill relaxes. "Who but Chacha could shave twice within the hour?"

Ivan moves his camera position to catch Chachaji shaving his other cheek.

Chachaji's cheeks have no cushion of flesh, and the blade sounds harsh and rasping against his skin and bone—rather like the sound of a barber sharpening his razor on a leather strap.

"It's great!" Bill whispers to me. "It's so Chachaesque."

Just when everyone thinks that Chachaji has finished, he goes on to shave his ears. Then he brings a small pair of scissors, with pink handles and with flowers painted on the blades, out of the tin and clips his pencil-line mustache. He rinses his face with the hot water from the cup and dries himself.

As Chachaji meticulously rewraps his razor blade and puts his things back in the tin, sounds of the Arya Samaj worshippers arriving for their morning prayers reach us from the front veranda. "Cut!" Bill calls out. The whole shaving ritual has taken no more than three minutes.

At Bill's prompting, I now give Chachaji a new shaving brush, a new safety razor, and some new blades—things that Chachaji, through my parents, had asked me to bring him from America. Bill had stopped me from giving them to him earlier, for fear he might use them in the shaving sequence and ruin its charm. But Bill's fear proves unfounded, because Chachaji admiringly strokes the plastic coverings of the presents and, without opening them, stores them away in the trunk under his bed, saying, in English, "Now I have all the facilities I need for shaving. Thank you." Then he turns to me and whispers, "Please give your Chachaji two rupees. His pockets are empty this morning."

"Does he now want money for sitting for his photograph?" Bill asks.

"Not precisely," I reply, and I explain that it is not Chachaji's way to make a direct connection between work and compensation, for fear he might give offense. As a rule, he does what people ask, and then relies on their good will.

"Let it be," Chachaji says quickly, perhaps mistaking my delay for reluctance. "It's not necessary just immediately."

I suggest to Bill that he give Chachaji some sort of daily allowance while we are shooting the film.

"How much? Two rupees a day?" he says. "That's a real bargain."

"I had in mind about fifty," I say. I think of mentioning a much bigger sum, but I know that Chachaji would have difficulty understanding a gift of even fifty rupees, since no one has ever given him that much money at one time before.

"Fifty rupees!" Bill exclaims, and then adds, "That's only about seven dollars. Why not? Cran Productions can afford that. But that's my limit."

He starts to hand Chachaji fifty rupees, but I intervene.

"No. It should be put in an envelope with his name on it."

Bill laughs.

(Every day from then on, Bill gives Chachaji fifty rupees, in an envelope with "Bahali Ram" written on it. Chachaji always locks the envelope away in his trunk, for the day when his grandson will need college tuition or his granddaughter a dowry.)

Bill and Ivan discuss the idea of filming Chachaji—possibly from above—as he putters around in the back courtyard. The first day or so, it bothered me that they talked about him as if he weren't there. Then I realized that he couldn't follow what they were saying, and really didn't have a clue to what was going on. (His innocence has its advantages: he is completely unselfconscious about the camera and always looks natural.)

Chachaji now suddenly says to me—as if Bill and Ivan were not there—"The Arya Samajists are praying. I had better go and pray with them." He shuffles off.

After the prayer meeting, Chachaji busies himself bolting and padlocking the door of his room.

"I am getting the immortal bed-tea scene in the can while the going is good," Bill says.

The custom of taking tea in bed before getting up dates from British times. My parents enjoy lingering over bed tea, especially now that Usha, Art, and Kate are staying in the house and can join them.

I ask Chachaji about filming him taking bed tea with my parents.

"It's getting very late," he says, in faint protest. "More photographs are not in my program. I must immediately take the milk to Madan for his tea."

"Tell him it's costing me eighty-two dollars an hour to have the crew wait around for him," Bill says. "His son can bloody well do without milk one more morning."

Editing Bill's remark, I tell Chachaji that as soon as we finish the bed-tea sequence Yoginder Singh will rush him and the milk to his son's house.

"Whatever you say," Chachaji says. "But tell Cran

Sahib that he has already taken a lot of photographs. What more is there left to see?"

At my parents' house, another problem develops. Usha declares that since Art can't be in the bed-tea scene, she doesn't want to be in it, either. But then Daddyji calls to her from the bedroom, and she goes in.

Chachaji starts agitating at my elbow. "Madan is not going to have milk for his tea. This is not a good program."

Usha emerges from the bedroom and says, with forced determination, "Bill, I want to be in the scene."

"Excellent news," Bill says. "I thought reason would prevail."

Ivan starts setting up the camera at the window in the rear of the bedroom. Daddyji and Mamaji, who have really already had their bed tea, and have been up for several hours, get back into their beds and try to look as if they were just waking up.

The houses in which my parents and Chachaji live are similar. They were both built after Partition, on small plots of land set aside by the government for refugees. But since Bill is interested in pointing up the contrast between my parents' station in life and that of Chachaji, he rearranges the furniture so that light will flood in on my parents through the window, making the room look much bigger than it actually is. When he staged Chachaji waking up, he contrived to make his room look smaller and dingier than it actually is.

I ask Bill if he isn't overdoing the contrasts and ignoring the similarities.

"You can't afford subtleties when you're scratching around for a story," he says.

Chachaji at the Arya Samaj Prayers

Jane puts up the board. As in real life, a servant enters the room with a tea tray and shyly exchanges Hindu greetings with my parents and Usha. Mamaji serves tea. Usha talks to Daddyji and gets him his morning newspaper. Chachaji arrives and is made welcome. Mamaji pours his tea, and Usha puts a lot of sugar in it, stirs it for him, and hands it to him. Mamaji then hands him a biscuit. He pops the entire biscuit quickly into his mouth.

Chachaji, Daddyji, and Usha look very natural in the sequence, but Mamaji looks strained. She knows Chachaji so well and sees so much humor in his little ways that she doesn't trust herself to keep a straight face for the camera.

MAMAJI MAKES EVERYONE Indian-style scrambled eggs—cooked with whole chilis, onions, and tomatoes—and *parathas*. Except for Sally, who has not taken to Indian cooking and, in any case, is not much of an eater, all of us eat heartily. We left the hotel early, and none of us have had anything but coffee.

Today is Sunday. Chachaji rings up Chopra to try to get tomorrow off, since otherwise he can't make the trip to Hardwar.

Mrs. Chopra answers the phone. "How is it that you are disturbing him on his day of rest?" she says sweetly to him, but he is quick to grasp the menace behind her voice.

Chachaji asks me to take the phone, and with me Mrs. Chopra becomes almost unctuous. "I can assure you that Chopra Sahib will have no objection," she says. "He wouldn't think of offending Mother Ganga and being on the wrong side of God. Say a prayer for us at the Ganga."

Yoginder Singh returns. He has spent two hours looking for Chachaji, and has stirred up the whole neighborhood to help him. He bawls out Chachaji for not being where he was supposed to be.

"Brother, I am supposed to be wherever I am," Chachaji says.

Yoginder Singh chuckles, and the two go off in the car to take the milk to Madan at last and, as Chachaji puts it, "to make arrangements for the milk for the day I will be bathing in the Ganga in Hardwar."

I busy myself on the telephone in the bedroom trying to get us rooms for our overnight stay in Hardwar. Because there are several women in our group and because my parents are coming along, Bill wants us to have Western-type accommodations, which are almost unheard of in Hardwar. The only possible place is called the Antibiotic Guest House. It belongs to Indian Drugs & Pharmaceuticals, Ltd., a government concern, and is seven miles from Hardwar. Since we aren't connected with the government, we don't technically qualify to stay there, but Mahesh uses his influence and is able to book us in.

I try to console Art for not being included in the dinner-table shots.

"Your friends seem to be trying to show the country in a bad light," he says. "It's all right to show Indian poverty, but you should also show Indian progress— like the sinking of new tube wells in the villages."

"Spoken like a Fulbright scholar!" Bill interjects,

filling his pipe. Art, who is studying anthropology and has done some work on a Punjabi village, is here on a Fulbright scholarship.

"Nowadays, lots of good Indian families have not one but two or sometimes three American members, or have children settled in the West," Umi says, joining in the discussion. She and Nimi have just driven over for a visit. "Two of my daughters have settled in the West with their Indian husbands. You should show that side of our family life, too."

"I don't think it would be fair to show Art in the picture and not show Kate," Nimi says. "In a sense, she is also part of our family."

"If Nimi had her way, our American tenant upstairs would be in the picture, too," Umi says, laughing. (The upper story of my parents' house is rented to an American.)

"I think the truth of the medium requires that I be in the film," Kate says earnestly. "You shouldn't just show an Indian family in black and white. You should show all the grays, too. I think it's significant that Daddyji and Mamaji have an American son-in-law and an American house guest, who are completely accepted and appreciated by the family. I don't feel at all strange calling them Daddyji and Mamaji."

"In a way, the family's acceptance of Kate and me is also a mark of Indian development," Art puts in. He returns to the theme of how misleading Western portrayals of Indian poverty are, and goes on to claim that the only convincing thing he has ever read about poverty in any underdeveloped country is Alan Paton's "Cry, the Beloved Country."

Araminta says that Paton is not literature.

Art says that if that particular book isn't literature, he'd like to know what is.

Art argues in the inspired tones of visiting American students, Peace Corps volunteers, and State Department apologists. Araminta, who has the air of a feminist and a left-wing intellectual, argues in the strident tones of an Oxford bluestocking. She is verbally dexterous, but Art is stubborn. (The argument about who should or should not be in our film—and what is or is not literature—is revived whenever we all get together, and becomes a sort of subtext to the discussions that Bill and I keep having about the Chacha film.)

AT NOON, WE SET OFF for Hardwar. Bill and Araminta squeeze into the station wagon with the crew, where Jane is sewing patches on the bluejeans she is wearing. Daddyji, Mamaji, Chachaji, Sally, and I all get into a large old Ford we have hired, with a new driver, named Ram Chandar. (Yoginder Singh is unavailable for a couple of days, and the Ambassador is too small for all of us.)

I tell Ram Chandar to keep the station wagon in view, but he's no Yoginder Singh, and even before we have passed the city limits we are separated from the station wagon.

Daddyji starts singing a childhood song about a wayfarer setting out on an open road that takes him where it would. Chachaji joins in. Normally, he speaks in a thin monotone, but his singing voice has considerable energy.

We reach the Antibiotic Guest House just after dark. The authorities have managed to come up with only six rooms, instead of the eight we requested. The rooms are modern and large, however, with Western-style bathrooms.

As we stand around on the veranda, Bill, Ivan, and Eoin fall to joking about who will room with whom. Everyone is in high spirits.

Bill says that as a special treat Chachaji should have the best room and have it to himself.

Sally, who has been on a tour of all the rooms, reports that the best room is the one nearest to where we are standing. Everyone urges Chachaji to take it.

Chachaji, who has never stayed in any kind of hostelry, seems confused. He looks at the room through the open door but won't go in. "This is too large," he says. "My place is not here. I'll stay with the drivers for the night, if you don't mind."

Sally says the smallest room is upstairs, and we all escort Chachaji up to it. Daddyji presses him to stay there, saying, "It will be a good experience for you, Bahali Ram."

Chachaji reluctantly agrees.

I tell Bill that the pilgrims in Hardwar usually bathe in the Ganges before sunrise—before they have eaten anything, and before they have fully opened their eyes on the world they regard as illusion. I suggest that perhaps we should all drive in to Hardwar before dinner and scout out possible locations, so as not to lose time in the morning.

"The crew are pretty tired," Bill says. "If I have to call them early in the morning, it would be good public relations to let them rest tonight."

"Hardwar under night lights would be exciting," Ivan says, happening to overhear us. "I want to go."

Everyone wants to go—even the drivers, who are eager to pay homage to the holy place right away. I prevail upon Daddyji to take a nap, but all the rest of us do go.

It seems that Hardwar doesn't sleep. The bazaars, ancient and gaudy, dirty and vulgar, are all open. They are crowded with pilgrims, mendicants, hawkers, lepers, holy men—walking, sitting, squatting, sleeping, singing, crying, whining, beseeching—who are jostled everywhere by cows, bullocks, handcarts, bicycles, even monkeys that drop down from the trees. The entire city smells of sweat and manure, of toil and death.

Bill surveys the whole scene enthusiastically and discusses with Ivan various spots and angles for shooting.

We are now standing at the top of flight after flight of white marble steps—called Har-Ki-Pauri, or God's Steps—that lead down to the river. A portly Brahman with a pockmarked face attaches himself to Mamaji, recognizing her as a soft touch. "Sister, you must make a prayer offering to Mother Ganga immediately. I will officiate."

Mamaji goes off with the Brahman down a little lane, returns with a large leaf, a candle, and a basket of jasmine blossoms—her prayer offering—and then follows the Brahman down Har-Ki-Pauri.

"How will I bathe in Mother Ganga without my own towel?" Chachaji suddenly asks me.

"Cran Productions has no provision in its budget for a towel," Bill says, laughing. "But because I'm such a sport I'll buy you one. But five rupees is the limit, Chacha, old boy."

Mamaji comes back up Har-Ki-Pauri, and we all go to look for a towel for Chachaji.

Bill stops in front of a stall and points to a red-and-green striped square of cloth. "What about that, Chacha? It'll look fabulous in the photograph."

Chachaji is not very keen on it. "The colors are not fast. It's very thin. It won't last."

"It has nice colors," Bill says. "It's this or nothing." In an aside to me, he says, "Remember the shoes? Once bitten, twice shy." Chachaji gave the shoes that Bill had bought him to his son, because he felt that, among other things, they were too good for him to wear himself.

"Let it be," Chachaji says, and he accepts the towel.

February 27th

D ADDYJI WAKES US ALL IN OUR HOSTELRY ROOMS AT five-thirty in the morning. We dress quickly, breakfast, and are ready to drive into Hardwar. Daddyji himself, however, is a little slow, partly because he has to take several kinds of medicine for his heart condition. Bill decides to go ahead with the crew in the station wagon.

"We'll just take some random shots of Hardwar and of pilgrims bathing," Bill says to me. "I don't think we'll need you. You can take your time bringing your parents."

I try to get him to wait. He and the crew have not done any Indian shooting on their own, and not one of them speaks a word of Hindi. Moreover, Hardwar is the citadel of the orthodox, for whom all foreigners are Untouchables or outcasts and therefore undesirable intruders. But Bill won't be detained, and goes off with the crew and Araminta.

I rush Daddyji along, and then he, Mamaji, Chachaji, Sally, and I drive as fast as we can to Hardwar.

We spot Bill and the crew standing on a bridge over a man-made channel near Har-Ki-Pauri. A man in a guard's khaki uniform is shouting at Ivan and gesticulating wildly. Then the man seizes hold of Ivan's camera, and before we can reach the bridge perhaps fifty religious men with holy stripes on their foreheads, all shouting and gesticulating, have surrounded Ivan, Bill, and Eoin. Jane and Araminta are standing off to one side.

"It's forbidden to take pictures of holy Mother Ganga!"

"It's sacrilege to bring a camera to this holy place!"

"Pilgrims come here, sick and lame. Their sorrow and grief are meant only for the eyes of Mother Ganga."

"Hand over the film!"

"The Untouchables have dishonored our people."

I fear for everyone's safety and worry about damage to the equipment, and I elbow my way into the crowd. I listen to everyone. I don't contradict anyone.

I don't argue. I have been in angry Indian crowds before and I know that one wrong word can turn even ordinarily peaceable citizens into a rampaging mob. Gradually, as I explain what we are doing, the people become somewhat mollified, and the realization that the foreigners are in the company of Indians helps. The man in the guard's uniform, however, refuses to let go of Ivan's camera, and insists on confiscating the film in it. Bill denies that Ivan has taken any pictures.

"Sahib tells a lie in the holy place," the guard says, his anger rising. "I saw it with my own eyes—that he took pictures."

The crowd starts getting worked up again.

I try to tell the guard politely that we have permission from New Delhi to take pictures, but he is not impressed.

I signal to the crew that we should get away from the bridge, and we start walking toward the cars. The guard lets go of Ivan's camera, but he and the crowd follow us, and he continues to demand the exposed film.

I go on talking softly to the crowd, and gradually its members drop behind and disperse.

We wait in the cars for a while, and then walk up to some higher ground, from which Ivan hurriedly tries to line up a shot with a telescopic lens.

"It's no good," Bill says, looking through the viewfinder. "We need real closeups of the pilgrims."

"It'll mean more trouble. But I suppose we don't really have any choice," I say.

Even before I finish speaking, several men in khaki

uniforms, followed by a much larger and more heterogeneous crowd than before, are upon us.

"Get these Untouchables out of here," a Brahman says to me angrily, pointing to the non-Indians in our group. "They are defiling our holy ground."

We try to leave, but can't escape the crowd. People are demanding that we go with them to the courthouse and surrender the exposed film. I am loath to get involved with the authorities and cause them to start a file on the case: to be caught in red tape here is to be a fly trapped in a spider's web—the more one turns and twists, the more firmly one is held. There is no way to shake off the crowd this time, however, so I accede to the demands.

I send my parents and Chachaji back to the cars for safety, and the rest of us allow ourselves to be marched down one lane and up another, until we reach a small stone barrackslike building. Bill and I go in, leaving the others and the equipment with the crowd at the door. They peer in as we are brought before the magistrate, who sits just inside. The magistrate has religious stripes painted on his forehead and sacred threads tied around one wrist; from these, and from the degree of deference shown him, it is clear that he also has a high religious position in the community. In fact, that is probably why he was made the holy city's magistrate in the first place.

"The city fathers have vested the ultimate authority for granting permissions in me," he announces, in very Sanskritized, florid Hindi. "All permissions from Delhi are invalid in the holy city."

The crowd, listening at the door, picks up and

repeats the line: "All permissions from Delhi are invalid in the holy city."

I respectfully request the magistrate to give us his permission to take shots of the pilgrims bathing in the river.

"First, you apply in writing; then I will decide," he says. "But once you have applied, if I reject your application there is no appeal."

It sounds peremptory and final—almost like "Off with his head!" But I go on talking. Then, finding that I have got nowhere, I submit a formal written application in simple English, spelling out the permissions we already have from the government, giving the background of the film, and begging the magistrate's permission to shoot in Hardwar.

He looks at the paper, and it becomes evident that he can't read English. He goes into a little trance, mumbles something, and then asks me, "What is the point of your film?"

I tell him about Chachaji, my old relative, and his lifelong wish to come to Hardwar, and about my wish to film him in a quiet, poetic way for the educational network in America.

The magistrate says, "You have my permission to photograph your relative—"

"Permission, permission," someone at the door says, and the word is picked up and runs like a continuous whisper through the crowd.

"And I will give you an escort to stay with you. But do your filming quickly."

I tell him that we will be out of Hardwar before noon.

The escort is an old man, barefoot and toothless, with a fat stomach, and with a holy man's tuft of hair hanging down the back of his otherwise shaven head. He wears a large, tightly buttoned khaki coat, which rides up over his fat stomach to hang loosely on his shoulders as he moves, and makes him look a bit like a vulture. He has the unlikely title of constable. But in the holy city his powers are magical. The crowd at the door falls back to make way for him and soon vanishes into the ancient streets. Bill is delighted, and dubs our escort "the walking permission slip."

We gather Mamaji, Daddyji, and Chachaji from the cars and proceed to Har-Ki-Pauri.

Chachaji walks along by my side, complaining all the time in a low drone. "Cran Sahib's towel is not adequate for the holy dip. It is too thin. It's not adequate for drying me."

Har-Ki-Pauri is thick with pilgrims, and the constable has to clear a path for us. Near the bottom of the marble steps, Ivan, camera in hand, perches himself precariously on top of a railing, with a clear view of the river. Eoin, who is not recording, because the sounds are too general and confused, stands with the rest of us on a nearby landing. The camera starts rolling, and I call out to Chachaji that he may now go down to bathe. We have not told him what to do or rehearsed him for this scene, because Bill has said he wants it *"au naturel."*

Chachaji shuffles down the marble steps, with the constable, in his ill-fitting coat, by his side. He stops on a landing a few steps above the water and, glancing hesitantly at the constable, modestly begins undressing. Before removing his trousers, he wraps around himself

Pilgrims and Venders in Hardwar

a pair of thin, worn, red-and-white checked bathing drawers he has brought along. Suddenly, he doesn't know what to do with his trousers. He starts to leave them on the step where he has put his other clothes and his towel, but then he changes his mind and shouts up to me, "Someone will steal them!"

"Brother, Mother Ganga will watch over your trousers," a Brahman busybody assures him. "Why do you worry? You could leave ten million rupees here and no one would touch them, because this is the bosom of Mother Ganga. Brother, you will find human beings who behave like animals everywhere else but not in the lap of Mother Ganga." The Brahman tries to take Chachaji's trousers from him.

"I'm glad to see that you are behaving like a gentleman," Chachaji says to him, refusing to let go of his trousers.

"Tell Chacha to get a move on!" Bill says. "We're burning up film."

I shout to Chachaji that his trousers will be safe, that everyone in the team will watch them devotedly, and that he should go ahead and take his bath.

Chachaji reluctantly puts down his trousers, and walks toward the water, his worn red-and-white checked drawers flapping around his thin body. He shivers a little. It's a cold morning, and the water, which comes down from the snowy mountains, is icy.

The river is a jumble of bobbing heads and quivering arms and legs. Hundreds of men, women, and children are bathing or pushing to get deeper into the river in order to immerse themselves from head to toe in its holy water. For a moment, we lose sight of Chachaji in the melee. When we spot him again, he is standing waist-deep in the river, taking water in his cupped hands and pouring it over his head. The current is strong. Chachaji totters, and falls into the water. He flails about and regains his balance, only to fall again.

"Oh, my God! He's drowning!" Bill cries out. "It's fabulous!"

The constable, who is standing fully clothed at the water's edge, rushes in after Chachaji.

"Ivan, are you getting all this?" Bill calls.

Ivan waves that he is, and continues shooting as Chachaji, shivering violently, is helped out of the water, sits down on the steps, and starts drying himself with his new towel.

"That was great!" Bill says. "Really great! Now can we get your mother bathing?"

"No, thank you," Mamaji says firmly. She quickly heads for a section of the river where only women bathe and no men are allowed.

Daddyji shouts after her not to stay in the water too long and get chilled.

"What about your father?" Bill asks.

"Not a chance," I say. Daddyji, unlike Chachaji and Mamaji, is not at all religious. Anyway, as a heart patient, he couldn't take the risk of bathing in such cold water.

"Jesus, to think we almost came here without old Chacha," Bill says. "We're lucky we brought him along or we wouldn't have had a bathing sequence at all. Can you imagine showing the Ganges without a bathing sequence?"

"You can thank Sally, Bill," I say. "You know, it

Eoin in Hardwar

was Sally who insisted that Chachaji should come along."

"Thanks, Sally," Bill says. "You're a real gentleman."

Chachaji, dressed again and clutching his wet towel, joins us. He looks very happy, for him.

"Well done, Chacha," Bill says.

We climb back up Har-Ki-Pauri.

At the top of the steps, we come upon a blind beggar who is just setting his tin cup down in front of him. He sings:

The boat is so old, and the shore is so far away.
Push away my sins, Lord Krishna.
My faith is my only support.
The truth is mine, the lie is mine, Lord Krishna.
We pilgrims have come to you, not with offerings of
    flowers but only with offerings of our tears.

"He would be a great mood-setter for Chacha's holy dip," Bill says to Ivan. Ivan has already started to shoot.

The sound of a coin dropped in the blind man's cup by a passerby lights up his previously expressionless face.

Chachaji is agitating for us to go and record the date of his ritual bath in the book of his *panda*. (A *panda* is a genealogist and a guide at a holy place.)

"What's so special about this book?" Bill asks. "Is the old boy hung up on files because he's a clerk?"

I explain to Bill that for hundreds of years the *pandas* have been entering in their books, among other things, the dates of pilgrims' ritual baths and the dates of the immersion of the ashes of the dead.

"God, we'd better humor the old boy, then," Bill says.

We find Chachaji's *panda,* a meek, obliging man, and film the genealogist, his subject, and his book—a long sheaf of very old paper, tied with hemp.

BACK IN Delhi, I tell Bill about a discovery I have made. In the course of desultory conversation in the car, Chachaji mentioned to me that he has two nephews living in a village called Amanpur, in the Punjab region, a few hours away from Delhi by train and bus, and that he visits them every two or three years—whenever he can spare seventeen rupees, for the cheapest railway ticket and the bus fare. I was elated to find that Chachaji had a village connection. It would help me persuade Bill to stay with the Chacha story, since we would now have an opportunity to film people much poorer than Chachaji himself.

"Fabulous!" Bill cries. "I'd like to see old Chacha, in his pink turban, hobbling around a destitute village. When do we go? Tomorrow?"

"We can't possibly go tomorrow," I say. "First, we have to see about getting Chachaji two or three days off. Chopra is not going to be happy about giving him another leave on top of the Hardwar day."

"You can handle that," he says. "You know how to function in India."

"I'm not so sure I know how to function with

Chopra," I say. "He's not the sort of man I'd seek out for a favor."

"You can do it," Bill says, in headmasterish encouragement. "I have faith in you. So we'll go to the village the day after tomorrow. I will give the crew tomorrow off and buy them a really good dinner, and then work them like dogs in the village."

February 28th

"YOU AND I HAVE TO DO A LITTLE BUSINESS WITH Som," I say to Bill. I tell him that there are many problems besides Chachaji's leave to be settled before we go to the village. A half-dozen foreigners cannot arrive in an Indian village without creating some social or political disturbance. We don't want to risk another episode like the one in Hardwar, so we must get an introduction to the local authorities. If we don't, the authorities will let us take pictures only of tube wells and tractors—symbols of progress, like what Art wanted us to film. There is also the matter of accommodations. Without the protection of a Western-type hotel or guest house, members of our group—especially since they lack the immunities of a native—could come down with dysentery or jaundice in a village, for the people there have no lavatories and use fields. We need to know how close a doctor schooled in Western medicine is to the village, in case of an emergency.

"Oh, God!" Bill says.

At the External Affairs Ministry, in between talking to a dozen other petitioners, Som promises to do "all the needful." Yes, his personal assistant will telephone Karnal—the biggest town near Chachaji's village—and get us into the National Dairy Research Institute Guest House, which, it seems, is the only hostelry with modern Western-type accommodations. Yes, he will send telegrams to state and district authorities. Yes, yes, yes.

I drop Bill at the Imperial Hotel swimming pool, and Yoginder Singh takes me on, in the Ambassador, to the post office, where I send telegrams to some unofficial contacts I have in Karnal. Hedging bets here is second nature to me. Then I drive to the Pharmacy of Prosperity to try to arrange for Chachaji's leave.

When I enter the Pharmacy of Prosperity, Chopra is typing, and he doesn't so much as look up. He has always had a suspicious, angry air, but today he seems positively malevolent.

I apologize for interrupting him, and then I put the case for Chacha's leave in the most personal terms. I tell him that I've been living abroad for nearly thirty years; that in that time I've seen very little of my relatives; that our film is intended as a homage to Chachaji—to the tenacity and dignity of one Indian.

"Who is stopping you from taking Bahali Ram?" he snaps. "I say take him not for a few days but for ten days or a month. I say take him with you to America."

"What I really want is assurances from you that

Chachaji will be able to come back to his job with you after two or three days' leave," I say.

"What businessman can give you such assurances these days?" Chopra says. "Haven't I already told you that he makes so many mistakes in his accounting that he's a liability to my business? He hinders its functioning." Pleased with himself, Chopra returns to his typing.

"I don't want Chachaji to lose his job just because he misses a little time."

"Maharaj," he says ironically, "I've already told you he can miss as many days as he likes. There is no job. I am only keeping him as a charity case."

Chopra abruptly summons Chachaji, who has been sitting outside the screen door poring over his ledger and listening to our conversation. "Ask him yourself right now if he wants to go to the village. If he says yes, you take him." Then he shouts at Chachaji, as if he were deaf, "Bahali Ram, you want to go to your village?"

"No, Chopra Sahib. I don't want to go anywhere. I just want to serve you and get your blessings."

"Am I stopping you from going to your village, Bahali Ram?"

"No, Chopra Sahib, you are not stopping me."

Chopra turns to me and shrugs. "What can I do?" he says. "He doesn't want to go to his village." He resumes typing.

I persist, for our whole film project may be in jeopardy.

"I've told you I'm only keeping him to give an old

man a little something to do," Chopra says. "Isn't that true, Bahali Ram? Didn't you already make two mistakes this morning, in the debit column?"

"Chopra Sahib, everybody makes mistakes," Chachaji says meekly.

"Everybody doesn't make mistakes every day," Chopra says.

"Chopra Sahib, you have spoken the truth," Chachaji says effusively. "I'm just getting old. My memory is going, my hand shakes. Chopra Sahib, you are absolutely right."

Exasperated, and somewhat mystified by Chopra's conduct, I go out to the Ambassador. On the one hand, Chopra makes out that Chachaji is useless, and, on the other, he implies that he can't spare him even for a short time. In theory, he could dismiss Chachaji at will, yet in practice he is very careful not to threaten, or even to seem to threaten, Chachaji with dismissal.

Yoginder Singh, who has been standing behind the gate talking conspiratorially to the bottle washer, comes running to the Ambassador. "Sahib, Chopra Sahib is a businessman," he says. "He has something you want, so you must give him something he wants. He's seen two cars pull up in front of his shop. He's seen the expensive camera. He's seen everything. He has eyes."

"I've already told you—no considerations, no bribes."

"Let me just go and tell him, Ved Sahib, that you belong to a very good Punjabi family, that there is nothing fishy about Sahib's film, that you are prepared to serve him in any honorable way."

I yield.

Yoginder Singh is gone for almost half an hour, and comes back clicking his tongue.

"Chopra Sahib doesn't listen to reason," he says. "It can be, Ved Sahib, that he is holding out for a big consideration, or it can be that Chopra Sahib is honest and wants nothing."

Back at the Imperial Hotel's outdoor café, the whole team, along with Araminta, is sitting family style eating lunch. Everyone is in the sun, and can't seem to get enough of it. The Indian lunchers all around them, however, constantly move their tables and chairs to stay in the shade.

I begin to tell about my ordeal with Chopra.

"What does Chopra pay him?" Bill asks. "Five rupees a day? What's that—sixty cents? That's nothing. Cran Productions can put him on a little pension."

"But, Bill, that's not the point," I say. "He must have his routine and the dignity of working."

"What the hell, he's eighty-three years old," Bill says.

Changing the subject, I ask Araminta how she is getting on with her article.

"I'd like to spend some time interviewing your American brother-in-law, Art, about Indian immigrants," she says.

"Yes, sure," I say. "Ring him up."

(This is the last we hear about Araminta's article. From here on, she goes everywhere with us, as if she were a part of the team.)

I decide to talk to Mahesh about the whole matter of Chachaji's leave. He has held several jobs in the public sector, and therefore might have come in contact with Chopra; the chemical business, like everything else here, is subject to hundreds of government regulations, requiring licenses. I go over to Mahesh's house and catch him just as he is finishing his lunch.

"I think I've heard of this fellow Chopra," Mahesh says. "He used to apply for all kinds of licenses to the State Trading Corporation when I was one of its directors. I didn't know until this minute that he was Chachaji's employer. I think he makes up his own powders and concoctions, puts them in old bottles with well-known brand labels on them, and sells them at a nice profit. For all I know, they may be as good as the brands he pretends they are, but it's still not cricket. He probably employs Chachaji because Chachaji doesn't know what's going on. If I were to give the word, my friends in the State Trading Corporation would launch an investigation, and Chopra would come here begging for mercy and the pleasure of employing Chachaji."

The last thing I want is to make trouble for Chachaji's employer, and Mahesh says that he feels the same way. We decide to try reason and persuasion again. This time, Nimi will come with me to the Pharmacy of Prosperity and talk to Chopra. If necessary, as a last resort, Yoginder Singh will drop a hint to the bottle washer that Nimi is the wife of the director of Indian Airlines, who has "long arms and a long reach." I am against that idea, but Mahesh insists that without applying some kind of pressure we may not be able to go on filming Chachaji at all. So I agree. In spite of myself, I am getting bogged down in the Indian morass: who you are; whom you know; what you know about whom; what hidden power you can mobilize. This seems to be the only recourse for anyone who wants to get things done here.

Chopra is no more forthcoming with Nimi there than he was with me alone.

"You tell me exactly what work Chachaji does for you," Nimi says to him, in her best well-bred-Punjabi manner, "and while he is away I'll either come and do his work for you myself or, if you think I'm not right for the job, I will arrange for my husband's accountant to come and do the work. I will arrange for a driver and car, and the driver will run for you all the errands that Chachaji runs for you."

"I am a businessman," Chopra says. "Bahali Ram is my employee. I have trained him to do certain tasks. How can you expect me to take the time to train your husband's accountant to do those tasks? Could your husband get along with an accountant I sent him? Can any business or office function like that?"

Young Chopra, who is busy in a corner with some bottles, looks through the screen door at the back and sees Yoginder Singh talking to the bottle washer. He goes out and joins them. Yoginder Singh makes sure that the elder Chopra notices them. Young Chopra then signals to his father, who gets up and goes out, and the two disappear behind the house.

"I think Yoginder Singh has dropped the hint about Mahesh's long reach," Nimi says.

Father and son soon return, and the son asks us abruptly whether we would like some coffee. I suddenly realize that in all my conversations with them they have never once offered me coffee or tea—a breach of Indian hospitality so glaring that only my long absence abroad could have made me overlook it.

"Daddy, what is the problem?" young Chopra says over coffee. "I myself will do Bahali Ram's work. I will run the errands. Let the poor man go to his village and enjoy himself for a couple of days."

"He must be here on Saturday to collect those forms from the income-tax office," Chopra says, making a show of firmness. He adds, almost pleadingly, "It's the last day for collecting those forms, and only Bahali Ram knows where to go and what to do."

Nimi and I assure him that, come what may, Chachaji will be there on Saturday. We hurriedly finish our coffee and leave.

Back at the hotel, Bill demands, "What time do we set out tomorrow? Is Chopra squared away?"

"Yes. We can go as early in the morning as you like."

"Fabulous," Bill says.

I start telling him some of the details of the encounter with Chopra, but he shows little interest. To him—at least, at that moment—Chachaji might have been an Indian plug or cable that had been obtained after some silly trouble and did not merit any further attention.

"Let's all go and have a bang-up Indian meal at Gaylord's tonight," he says, and while he is saying it Jane appears, dressed in an attractive khaki suit and espadrilles and doused with lots of perfume—all ready for an evening out.

"This is turning out to be a super day," Bill says.

March 1st

WE LEAVE FOR AMANPUR AT SEVEN-THIRTY, TAKING Yoginder Singh and the Ambassador as well as the station wagon. Bill rides in the Ambassador with Chachaji, Sally, and me. We are travelling due north, and the landscape becomes rural much more rapidly than it did on the way to Hardwar, off to the east.

"It looks as if we were really going to a village," Bill says enthusiastically.

We arrive in Karnal in about two and a half hours. It is a dairy center, with more than its share of Indian flies. Its most important landmark seems to be the large complex of newish buildings that make up the National Dairy Research Institute.

The accommodations clerk at the Dairy Research Institute Guest House, where Som had supposedly booked us, tells me, "No message, no telex, no telegrams have been received at this office. Just at present, there is a three-day dairymen's conference here, and every available room is booked."

I ask to see the head of the institute itself, and I am presented to a pleasant-looking man named Sunderam, who is an agriculturalist from South India. He listens sympathetically to the story of our predicament, and then asks the accommodations clerk how many rooms are still unoccupied.

"Four, sir," he says. "But they're reserved."

"Government regulations allow me to release reserved rooms to emergency guests if the rooms have not been occupied by nine-thirty in the morning," Sunderam says to me. "It's now ten o'clock. You can have the four rooms."

❧

YOGINDER SINGH drives very fast toward the village, even though the road is slippery as a result of several days' rain, which is continuing. When Bill suggests that we slow down, Yoginder Singh says, "Bill Sahib, don't worry. I've never had an accident." Then he urges Chachaji to be sure to tell him well in advance when to turn off for the village. But Chachaji doesn't seem to know the turning, and Yoginder Singh keeps on at him: "Is this it, Chacha? Is this where we turn?"

Suddenly, Chachaji calls out, "Turn!"

Yoginder Singh jams on the brakes and tries to make a right turn. As he does so, we hear a crash behind us. We stop and get out of the car.

"Chacha, are you riding in a car or on a mule?" Yoginder Singh shouts. "You can't turn a car like a mule!"

We discover that as the station wagon tried to follow Yoginder Singh into the turn, it was hit from behind by an Indian-made Fiat. Amarjit Singh is retrieving his turban from the muddy road and yelling at the driver of the Fiat, "You hit my turban right off my head!"

The Fiat driver, a mild-mannered fellow, guiltily

mutters, "I couldn't help it. The rains have ruined my brake drums."

Araminta tells Bill to take the Fiat's license number. Then Ivan notices that there are two passengers trapped in the back seat of the Fiat. He runs to help them, yanking at the doors first on one side, then on the other. But both doors are stuck, so he empties the boot of several bags of flour and potatoes, which had rolled forward with such force that the back of the rear seat had come loose and pinned the passengers under it.

Chachaji shuffles off in the rain and disappears behind a tree, without waiting to know the fate of the passengers.

Ivan pulls the two passengers out, through the boot. They are numbed but not hurt. The station wagon has only a dent in the right rear bumper. The Fiat, however, is pretty nearly wrecked. We are finally able to leave its driver and passengers in the care of some policemen who happen along in a lorry, and we continue our journey down the road that Chachaji told us to turn into.

The road becomes a muddy lane.

"Chacha, where is the village?" Yoginder Singh shouts.

"Brother, just keep driving," Chachaji says. Then he suddenly cries, "Here! Turn! No, stop!"

Yoginder Singh swerves the car to the right and then back, just in time to save us from landing in a marsh.

On our left, down a muddy slope, is the village of

Amanpur. Our cars have been sighted, and curious villagers run up the slope to stare at us.

We all get out and pick our way through the mud down to the village, Chachaji leading, and Yoginder Singh and Amarjit Singh following at a slight distance, trying to fend off the growing crowd of villagers. It is drizzling slightly, and the earth smells of manure and wet cattle.

Ivan takes some hasty miscellaneous shots.

A polite man, with the self-confidence of someone who knows how to talk to city people, joins us. He is Om Prakash, a village landlord. I tell him about the film, and he immediately takes a proprietary interest in it and insists on being our guide.

We skirt a cow pasture and a small schoolhouse; cross a footbridge over a water-filled ditch in which a few cows are lackadaisically drinking; make our way through a group of water buffalo chomping on refuse; and, after passing idle bullock carts, piles of manure, little storage houses filled with cakes of dried dung, mud huts, wandering chickens, brick houses, and more mud huts, arrive at the homes of Chachaji's nephews—two small, unfinished brick houses standing side by side at the bottom of a muddy track. Many of the village children have raced ahead to tell of Chachaji's coming, and women and more children come running toward us. The women surround Chachaji and touch his feet, then immediately pull back and cover their faces with their veils, as if they had belatedly become aware of our presence.

I learn that both of Chachaji's nephews are away on business, that two of the women are their wives,

Outside the Nephew's House in the Village
Left to right: Villagers, Bill, Chachaji, Sally, Eoin

and that a third, a very old woman, is Chachaji's long-widowed sister-in-law. The women invite us into one of the houses to have tea.

We step up onto a dried-mud veranda, which serves as both storage place and kitchen. At one end of the veranda, some chickens are scratching among piles of wood and cakes of dung; at the other, a fire of wood and dung is smoking from under a makeshift brick oven. The women lead us into a room off the veranda. (The house has three rooms in all.) It has one small window, and its walls are lined with outdated, luridly colored calendars picturing girls, goddesses, and landscapes, and with shelves displaying rows of brass trays, bowls, cups, and saucers. The utensils and pottery are arranged with military precision, and appear dusty and unused. Sticking incongruously out of each of the teacups is a light bulb, looking like a fragile bubble. The bulbs, I conclude, were probably bought in a fit of enthusiasm for the day when the house would have electric light.

The women have some of us sit on the charpoy, which is covered with a blue-and-white plaid cotton spread, and the rest of us on wooden chairs, with white woven plastic seats, that they have hastily carried in from the veranda. Then they busy themselves heating milk, mixing it with tea leaves in a brass urn, and spooning the tea into tall brass tumblers. They ceremoniously present each of us with two boiled eggs, taken straight out of a steaming pot. The eggs are so fresh—they were probably laid this morning—that none of us, except Chachaji, can peel them. The women laugh at our struggles, take the eggs from us, and quickly peel them with their fingernails. We sprinkle salt and chili powder over the peeled eggs and eat them appreciatively.

The room is too dark for filming, and Ivan asks the women, in pantomime, if there are any electrical outlets. The women say that they think they have seen one in the house of the other nephew, next door, and we all go there to check. Sure enough, it has an electrical outlet, but without wires.

"I think they have to plaster it before putting lightning into it," Chachaji's elderly sister-in-law tells me.

"We'll film in this house, because the natural light is better," Bill says. "But first let's restage the arrival scene and shoot that."

Bill tells me to tell the women and children what to do, and to ask Om Prakash and a cousin of his—another landlord, who has joined us—to play the part of Chachaji's nephews.

I tell Bill that Chachaji's nephews are contractors who recruit landless peasants for landlords, and are therefore of much lower social status than Om Prakash and his cousin.

"I tell you, on film they will all look like rustics," Bill says.

Eoin mutters something about keeping documentaries pure and truthful. "Documentaries should show only events that really happen and show them only as they are happening," he says, harping on a favorite theme. "You can always tell a bad documentary—the camera is in the room before a person enters instead of coming into the room with that person."

"That's just bad staging," Bill says. "In my opinion, whatever looks good, or can be made to look good, is fine in a documentary."

"Ha!" Ivan snorts. "That's straight out of the shortest book in the world—'The Journalist's Book of Ethics.'"

Bill laughs.

Yoginder Singh is in his element—waving and shooing away the crowd of gaping villagers, who have probably never seen any kind of camera before, let alone a large motion-picture camera.

Bill calls for Jane to bring the clapperboard, and we start filming. For the second time, Chachaji walks in the rain toward the houses of his nephews. The women and children emerge from the houses, giggling and enthusiastic in their feigned greeting.

Then Chachaji enters the house with the better natural light and sits down on the charpoy while the women and Om Prakash and his cousin gather around him in a circle on the floor and gaze up at him, as Bill has directed them.

Chachaji spontaneously recites some elegant Urdu couplets, and laughs and talks indulgently with his poorer relations, much as his better-off relations laugh and talk with him. He looks very happy in the role of sophisticated city dweller bringing enlightenment to country cousins.

The women on the floor inquire after sons of theirs who have gone to Delhi to seek their fortune and have reached marriageable age.

"It looks great," Bill says. "We see old Chacha in a mood here that we've never seen him in in the city. He's really somebody here."

The rain lets up, and Bill suggests that we leave Chachaji with his family and go off in different directions in order to elude the crowd. Ivan and Bill steal away to take some random mute shots of the village. Eoin and Jane start on a sightseeing tour. Araminta sets out on what she calls "a country walk." Sally and I return to the cars.

A huge crowd is standing staring at the cars as if they were flying saucers.

Ivan and Bill soon join us.

"Random shots are impossible," Ivan says. "Wherever I go, people follow me. And I can't make myself understood. We need the benefit of your Punjabi."

The rain has stopped, and Bill, Ivan, Sally, and I head back to the village, with the inevitable crowd tagging along. A young man who tells us, in English, that his name is English Singh attaches himself to us.

"Are you called English Singh because you can speak English?" I ask.

"No. I learned to speak English because I was called English Singh," he says.

"Are you a student?" I ask.

"I'm the only villager who has ever gone to college, and I went to college because I can speak English."

"But how did you learn your English?" I persist, trying to solve the conundrum.

"My name is English Singh."

Ivan slips away while English Singh sets about showing us the few village shops: the greengrocer's, whose total merchandise is one small basket of tired old carrots on the floor; the *pan* and cigarette shop;

which has no goods at all but in which six old, rather disreputable-looking men are sitting around a table playing cards; the cobbler's shop, which does have a few clogs but no customers; the outlet for Bata shoes—ostensibly a mark of prosperity in an Indian village—which is thronged with people who seem to be only admiring the shoes, not buying them.

Ivan rejoins us. He is more cheerful, because he has managed to get a few shots of villagers' faces. "I could spend a month here just taking pictures," he says.

It's the first time I've heard him sound enthusiastic about the film. Maybe the tide is turning in its favor, I think with some relief.

We return to the cars, which are now encircled by children who have been let out of school. They just stand there staring at the vehicles.

"I can't get over how passive Indian children are—not just here but in Delhi, too," Jane says to me. "When we were shooting in Egypt, the children would catch hold of our equipment, climb all over us and the cars, hang on to my handbag. They were so active and curious. They were always asking questions, not just about what we were doing but about where we had come from—about everything. And they were so helpful! They were always offering to carry camera magazines."

"You're right about the passivity," I say. "But children here are hungry. That's why they're so passive."

"I can't bear to think about it."

Chachaji comes walking up and asks me quietly, "Can I spend the night with you in the guest house?

Here, every time I have to go to the bathroom I have to go outside. The room you got me in Hardwar was a memorable place."

Bill overhears the last phrase, which Chachaji says in English, and cries, "What did I tell you? How you gonna keep 'em down on the farm after they've seen Paree?"

Chachaji is embarrassed that Bill might have understood his request, and he quickly says, "Never mind. Let it be. I will remain in the humble village."

"No, no. We'll take you back with us to the guest house," I say.

Meanwhile, Bill has decided that he wants another shot of Chachaji walking down to the village as if he were just arriving. But Bill doesn't want the children in the shot, so he tells them that Ivan will take their picture if they run over to the marsh and keep very still. They do as he says, and Ivan pretends to take their picture. Bill tells them to keep still for another picture, with Chachaji.

Ivan quickly turns the camera on Chachaji, and Bill shouts, "Chacha, walk toward the village and don't stop till I tell you to."

At one point, Chachaji's path is blocked by a large mud hut, and, to Bill's horror, Chachaji disappears behind it instead of going around the front, where the camera could follow him. It's beginning to rain again, and the light is fading. I dispatch the most alert-looking boy to tell Chachaji to pick up the path on the other side of the hut. Ivan quickly adjusts his camera to film the continuation of the walk. Bill is relieved—but only momentarily, because when Chachaji comes into view the boy is tailing him and staring back at the camera the whole time. Because the shot looks so good, Ivan continues shooting, in the vain hope that the boy will get bored and look away. But he never does.

"That bloody kid!" Bill exclaims. "That would have been such a lovely shot."

As we stand discussing whether to do another take of the walk, no one notices that Chachaji, obeying Bill's instructions to the letter, has gone on walking and disappeared into the village.

"The fool won't stop until he's right inside his nephew's house," Bill says. "He probably thinks we're still taking his photograph."

Bill runs down to the cow pasture to see if he can call Chachaji back, but it's too late. He shouts to me to send someone to fetch Chachaji. I shout back that we have tired Chachaji out and should give him a little rest.

"The old boy can jolly well walk another fifty yards!" Bill shouts.

Before I can argue the point with him, he sends English Singh off to fetch Chachaji. There is a sudden heavy downpour. The crew members run to the cars with the equipment. Bill starts running for the cars, too, but slips and falls in the mud. He picks himself up and comes limping toward us.

"I think I've broken my ankle," he says, panting in pain. "Yoginder Singh, take me back to Karnal at once."

Everyone is very solicitous. Then Sally remembers that Chachaji wanted to go back with us, and asks whether we shouldn't wait a few minutes for him.

"My ankle!" Bill cries. "Yoginder Singh, Karnal!"

We speed away, and Amarjit Singh and the crew follow us automatically in the second car, as if in a convoy—leaving Chachaji to puzzle out why we sent for him in the rain and then left without saying anything to him.

Back at the guest house, where everybody looks at Bill's ankle, it is found to be ominously swollen.

"It's probably just a nasty sprain," Araminta says. "If you keep it raised, it will be all better by morning."

Yoginder Singh looks at Bill's ankle closely and pronounces, "As Guru Nanak is my witness, there is no fracture. I am a wrestler, and I know about this kind of injury. Just let me heat up some oil and massage it into Bill Sahib's ankle, and he will be running around like a village chicken tomorrow."

Bill shows interest in Yoginder Singh's home remedy, but only for a moment.

I have little difficulty in persuading Bill to see a doctor once I emphasize that the shooting schedule will be disrupted if he is laid up. Araminta thinks that I am fussing too much, but I have my way, and Sally and I take Bill to a doctor who is attached to the institute and lives in the compound.

"I do not think the Englishman's ankle is broken," the doctor says after examining Bill in his drawing room. "But since he's an Englishman, I think it should be X-rayed." He gives us prescriptions for some ointment for the swelling and some pain-killing tablets, and sends us to an X-ray shop in the bazaar.

Yoginder Singh mutters all the way to the bazaar,

"A little hot oil, and in minutes I will have Bill Sahib's ankle fixed."

"That's right, and I'll never walk again," Bill mutters.

The X-ray shop turns out to be an open stall, with an open drain in front of it. "I will take a nice photograph of your ankle, which you will be proud to keep," the X-ray man says.

He develops the X-ray in less than ten minutes and holds it up, dripping, for Bill to see. He and Bill study it intently.

"No fracture," the X-ray man announces triumphantly.

"If my ankle had been broken, I'd have boiled Chacha in your hot oil, Yoginder Singh," Bill says. "It was all his fault."

March 2nd

WE ARRIVE IN THE VILLAGE ABOUT NINE O'CLOCK. Even before the cars stop, we are surrounded by a crowd of staring villagers. We start out by doing another take of Chachaji walking down to the village. (He spent the night in the house of one of his nephews.) The entire walk has to be refilmed, because it's now a clear morning, and the light is quite different from the hazy, overcast light of late yesterday afternoon.

Bill, whose ankle is no longer bothering him,

again positions Chachaji and tells him to start walking. Halfway down the path, four or five mangy dogs are going after one another.

"Bill, look!" Sally says. "Chachaji will walk straight into that dogfight."

"That would be really exciting," Bill says. "Maybe they will make the old boy wave his arms about imperiously, and that would certainly be a nice change from his usual stoic plod-along."

Sure enough, as Chachaji approaches the dogs he does wave his arms about imperiously. The dogs ignore him.

"Great walk, Chacha!" Bill calls out. "Now come back." Bill has spotted, coming slowly up the road toward us, a sort of trap, drawn by a shrunken, emaciated horse.

"It's perfect," Bill says. "Let's have Chacha arrive in that contraption."

Chachaji protests. "Cran Sahib knows that I take the bus as far as the dirt road and then I come on my legs," he says.

"But it will make a beautiful photograph, Chacha," Bill says. Turning to me, he adds, "That horse is Chachaesque par excellence. They bear an uncanny resemblance to each other."

Eoin again mutters something about staging events in a documentary.

I ask Chachaji if in real life he could ever expect to get a lift in such a trap. He reluctantly admits that it is not impossible. I hire the driver of the trap for the shot, giving Chachaji the money for the driver and coaching him in what Bill wants him to do.

Ivan starts shooting, and the trap, with Chachaji in it, clatters along the road toward the camera for about two hundred yards and stops at an appointed place, between two stones. The driver jumps down, and Chachaji climbs out of the trap. Chachaji gives the driver the money. As the driver turns his trap around and goes on his way, Chachaji starts his walk down to the village yet again.

"Excellent!" Bill cries. "This is my favorite shot so far, barring none. Chacha, you're a hero! Stop! Come back!"

Chachaji complains to me, "It is not a suitable carriage. Cran Sahib should have chosen a better-looking horse for the photograph. The horse is not right for a gentleman."

Everyone laughs.

"Let it be," Chachaji says, joining in the laughter a bit sheepishly.

It is a day of soft, bright light, and Ivan is impatient to get some general shots of the village. We walk around taking shots of villagers and village scenes.

"I've had it with the village," Bill suddenly says. "While the light is good, let's go to Karnal and do a shot of Chacha arriving on a train, and then let's get back to Delhi."

I tell Bill that I admire him for being so economical in his use of film stock—he hardly ever takes a shot without having a sequence in mind or an idea about how he will end up using it. But I also tell him that I feel he has rushed through the village sequences and relied on standard situations.

"Don't worry," he says. "I'll do quick cuts back

and forth from general village scenes to Chacha. The cuts will give the impression that we've kept the camera on Chacha the whole time he's been in the village."

As we are getting into the cars, all of Chachaji's country cousins—including his two nephews, who have just returned home—suddenly materialize, as if the news of our imminent departure had been broadcast by a village crier. Chachaji says farewell to them all, we thank everyone, and the cars roar away.

In the Ambassador, I get my first real chance to talk to Chachaji since we first came to the village.

"How did you like being in the village?" I ask him.

"I have enjoyed my visit very well," he says. "I personally thank Cran Sahib for it."

"Would you like to live there?" Bill asks.

"No. Village life is very boring."

Everybody in the car laughs.

Our stays in the village were so short and we were so busy getting the material Bill wanted that there was no time to find out what Chachaji did when he wasn't being filmed. I ask him about it now.

"I went to see my swami," he says. "Swamiji always remembers me. He always asks after me. Swamiji is so old, and yet he never forgets."

"How old is he?" I ask.

"Swamiji is a ninety-year-old gentleman. We spent a nice time saying mantras together in the temple."

To Bill, I say, "It's too bad we missed filming Chachaji and his swami. We didn't even know about the village temple."

"Damn," Bill says.

A Bullock Cart

"What else did you do?" I ask Chachaji.

"I walked through the village, and all the shop-keepers remembered me and greeted me with respect."

"That would probably have made a good scene, too," I say to Bill.

"Damn," Bill says again.

"Shall we go back?" I ask.

"I'd like to," Bill says. "But the crew have been crying hunger. Jane must have mentioned lunch six times. And it is three o'clock. Lugging a camera, camera magazines, a tripod, and a tape recorder is as draining as cutting hay, you know." No one wanted to eat lunch in the village, for fear of getting sick.

"What about taking an extra day for the village?" I ask.

"I agree with Chacha—it's a boring place," Bill says. "I want to get on to some new material. Let's have a quick lunch and do the arrival shot on the train and get on the road to Delhi before dark." It is dangerous to drive here after dark, for India has few of the services associated with driving in the West.

"Perhaps it's just as well we didn't get the old swami on film," Bill says now, trying to rationalize the lost opportunity. "We already have too many ritualistic sequences."

As we approach the guest house, the bearer and the cook can be seen standing outside looking anxiously up the road. "The Sahibs were expected for lunch two hours ago—did you have an accident?" the bearer asks. Punctuality is here thought to be one of the main characteristics of someone with a white skin, and the bearer and the cook can't imagine that white sahibs and memsahibs would be late without a very good reason.

We sit down in the dining room, everyone except Sally eager for a good Indian meal. No one is in the least prepared for what the bearer and the cook serve us—pork chops, mashed potatoes, and peas, all covered with thick brown gravy.

"Rhubarb! Rhubarb!" Bill cries in disappointment.

"'Shame! Shame!' is what he means," Araminta says.

A pall settles over the table. We eat quickly, pack our bags, tip the bearer and the cook, and race to the station to film the five-fifteen train from Delhi.

"In the film, we'll show a shot of the train arriving, right?" Bill says. "We'll show a shot of Chacha coming out of the station, right? Then we can cut to Chacha in the trap and Chacha walking down into the village. That will be the whole journey sequence."

"But we won't have shown him actually on a train," I say.

"That's true. Well, then, after we film Chacha coming out of the station we'll all get on the train and Ivan can do some tracking shots. Yoginder Singh and Amarjit Singh can pick us up at the next station."

As soon as we arrive at the station, we put into effect a plan that Bill and I have worked out to distract the inevitable crowd. Bill, Chachaji, and I go inside the station while all the others sit casually in the cars, which are immediately surrounded by the curious. After a minute or so, Bill saunters out of the station alone, drawing a crowd with him toward the cars. While Bill holds the crowd's attention, Ivan darts out and sets up his camera near the entrance to the station. I then tell Chachaji to walk out of the station and past a couple of leprous beggars, past two or three broken-down pushcarts, and up to a few tongas—horse-drawn carriages—that stand a hundred yards away from the gate. We need the tongas to help create the illusion that Chachaji hires the trap in Karnal.

For once, everything goes smoothly, and Ivan is able to film Chachaji emerging from the station and arriving at the tongas.

All of us enter the station. The stationmaster doesn't insist on the punctilio of official permissions for filming the train. In fact, he allows us to wait with him in his office, away from the crowd of oglers. It's five o'clock, and the train from Delhi is due at five-fifteen, but he has not yet received the signal telling him which of the tracks—there are two—the train will arrive on. Bill and Ivan, however, have singled out a site on a bridge with a good view of both tracks.

"As soon as Ivan has taken a shot of the train coming in, he'll race down and get on the train," Bill says.

I tell Bill that the more of us there are on the train, the more likely we are to get mobbed, and that in the confines of a train compartment it may be impossible to do shooting at all.

"Then just you and Sally should get on the train with Ivan," Bill says. "You can interpret for him, and Sally can put up the board. The rest of us will rush up to the next station in the cars."

Bill puts the idea to Ivan, but Ivan rejects it out of hand. He refuses to do any shooting without Jane, probably because he feels protective toward her as his assistant and doesn't want any of her duties to be usurped. Bill, sensing union-type problems, quickly yields, and turns to Eoin. Predictably, Eoin insists that, as a good sound man, he must record how the train sounds from inside the compartment at exactly the moment Chachaji is being filmed in it. Bill then decides that if everybody else is going to be on the train, he should also be there, to direct.

"Araminta and Sally can go in the cars," Bill says. "That will at least be two fewer people."

"Nothing doing," Araminta says, loudly and emphatically. "I've never been on an Indian train, and I'm certainly not going to be left behind. Sally can go with the cars."

Bill immediately goes to the ticket window and comes back with seven first-class tickets to Bahani, the next station—tickets for all of us except Sally, who stands in a corner looking resentful.

"What about a ticket for Sally?" I ask Bill.

Bill looks sheepish. "She can be in charge of the cars."

"But she feels displaced," I persist.

"It's a goddam insurrection." Bill walks away in exasperation.

I reflect that there is no demonstrable need for Ivan to take Jane, or, indeed, any camera assistant; that Eoin could tape the inside sounds of a train some other time; that Araminta could find plenty of other opportunities to ride Indian trains; that there is no necessity for Bill to direct a simple train sequence; but that by now we are a makeshift family, with its own minor rivalries, not to mention a certain amount of protectiveness among the men toward the various women. Only Chachaji, who apparently still does not understand the nature of our enterprise, seems to be outside the dynamics of this little family. He seldom asserts his preferences—in fact, doesn't seem to have many, as if he felt that having preferences was a right of the well-to-do.

I go and buy a ticket for Sally. The stationmaster rushes over to me and says, "Hurry, hurry! I've just got the signal. The train is coming on Track 2. It will stop here for only a couple of minutes."

Ivan races up onto the bridge, and the rest of us run out onto the platform. The train is just coming in. It is, however, on Track 1, not Track 2.

"Goddam Indians! They can't even get their train signals straight," Bill says, waving furiously up to Ivan to turn the camera onto Track 1. Then he notices that Ivan is already shooting the train. "I've never known a more agile cameraman. I'll give him A-plus every time."

When the train stops, Bill wants to find the first-class compartment, but there is such a rush of passengers, lugging steel trunks and bedrolls, baskets and bundles, that we all scramble into the first compartment we come to that has empty seats, Ivan dashing in from behind just as the train pulls out.

Chachaji sits next to the window, and Ivan on the aisle seat next to him, so that he can film Chachaji looking out the window at the passing countryside. As soon as people notice Ivan's camera, they push and crowd into our compartment. Most of them are men, and they soon become unruly. They taunt Jane, Sally, and Araminta—foreign women are fair game—calling out things like "She's a lovely!" and "Catch her, catch her, and take her home!" Whenever I translate an instruction to Chachaji, they chant after me, "Chacha, Chacha, Chacha . . . Camera, camera, camera." They press against us, trying to touch the women and the camera. Bill, Eoin, and I stand in the aisle to form a sort of shield, but we have difficulty holding the crowd back. To keep the camera out of the crowd's reach, Ivan and Chachaji switch seats.

Ivan now leans out of the window and tries to film the passing countryside. Some boys in the compartment ahead hang out of its window shouting, "Camerawallah, look this way!"

"I wish they'd fall off the train!" Bill says. "How can he shoot with them in the way?"

Ivan doesn't respond to the shouts, and eventually the boys tire and draw back into their compartment. At last, Ivan is able to take a few shots of the countryside.

The countryside is flat and green. The grass looks unusually lush. It glistens from the recent rains.

The train slows down, as if it were about to stop at a station, but nothing can be seen ahead except a few goats grazing.

"Is this Bahani?" I ask the people around us.

"Bahani! Bahani!" they start chanting. "Hurry! Hurry! Jump! Train only stops five seconds!"

It is difficult to get to the door, for people, trunks, bedrolls, baskets, and bundles are everywhere. Bill is the first to scramble over the obstacles and jump out. Chachaji, used to making his way through crowds, is next. The train starts to move, and Sally and I have to

Chachaji on the Train

jump off hurriedly. Araminta is right behind us. Then we hear Jane scream, and Sally spots her lying on the ground flat on her face.

"Someone on the train pinched me and pushed me off!" Jane cries, picking herself up. "They're all disgusting."

Eoin and Ivan jump off the train as it gathers speed. No one is hurt, but everyone is a little shaken.

We are not sure where we are. For all we know, we've been tricked into getting off in the middle of nowhere. Then, to our relief, Yoginder Singh and Amarjit Singh come running toward us. They lead us a couple of hundred yards up the line, past the goats and some goatherds' huts, and across the tracks to the two cars.

Bill decides to ride in the station wagon, for once, with Araminta and the crew, wanting either to register disapproval of Sally or to settle the others down. Chachaji, Sally, and I get into the Ambassador.

Before either car can be started, the sky darkens—so swiftly that later the local people cannot remember a precedent for it, even during the monsoons. Within seconds, it's night, and big drops of rain pelt the ground. Yoginder Singh switches on our headlights, revealing a silhouette of Ivan stretched out in the back of the station wagon filming the storm.

"Ved Sahib, we should get going," Yoginder Singh says. "This is the kind of storm that no one should take chances with."

"We'll have to wait until Ivan Sahib finishes filming," I say.

"I know this country, Sahib. This is dangerous. I have known the roofs of Ambassadors to cave in."

There is a series of rapid-fire explosions in the sky, followed by a deep, sustained rumbling. We can make out Eoin's arm holding the microphone out of the window. Within moments, hailstones, some of them two inches across, are pounding the roof of the car.

Yoginder Singh blesses himself and shouts to me over the unnatural clatter, "Sahib, I don't think this roof can last! But now there is no question of driving, either!"

We fall silent.

After a while, Yoginder Singh says, "No one would have had time to bring the cattle into the houses. All the cattle outside will be dead. Even people will die."

Sally looks toward me, as if she had full confidence that I wouldn't have got her into the middle of the storm without knowing how to protect her. In a way, I have a similar confidence in Yoginder Singh. Chachaji sits passive and unconcerned.

"If we stay here, Sahib, we'll die," Yoginder Singh says.

I roll down the window and shout to Bill that we must get going and look for shelter.

Yoginder Singh starts inching forward, and as Armajit Singh waits for us to pass, we can just make out that a bottle is being passed around in the station wagon. Nothing can be seen ahead or on either side of the road, and the beating of the hailstones on the thin metal roof of the car is deafening. Sally and Chachaji are very quiet.

After ten minutes, we come to the main road and a little shack—a sort of coffee shop *cum* petrol station— but it is closed. Someone, however, has left a light burning, so we decide to wait near it. The station wagon draws up alongside.

We sit for about fifteen minutes, during which the fury of the hailstorm doesn't abate. Then Bill rolls his window down and shouts through the lashing hail, "I think the storm is letting up! How about going on to Delhi?"

"You're joking!" I shout back. "We'll be drowned in the floods!"

But Bill has already rolled his window up, and the station wagon is pulling out.

Yoginder Singh rolls his window down and grabs the door handle of the station wagon, yelling to Amarjit Singh to stop. (The station wagon has the left-hand drive of an American car, and the Ambassador has the right-hand drive of an Indian car.)

Amarjit Singh yells back, "The sahibs have drunk a lot of whiskey and are telling me to drive to Delhi!"

I tell Amarjit Singh to ignore that order, and for a few minutes we sit without moving, in uneasy silence.

Then the storm does seem to let up slightly, and Yoginder Singh says he thinks that it would be safer to try to reach the guest house than to wait the storm out any longer on the road.

Slowly, with Yoginder Singh blowing the horn all the way, we find our way back to Karnal and the guest house. Its electricity has been knocked out, and it looks forlorn, but we are glad to see the bearer and the cook, who make us feel welcome.

The violent, relentless clatter of hailstones on the roof and the windows of the guest house has the force of some primitive assault, but we feel protected by the candlelit drawing room. The room is built on a grand colonial scale, and the candles, slender and small, light up an armchair here, a table there, a figure here, a figure there. Ivan peers out of the window into the storm. His bearded silhouette against the pane could be the bust of a Biblical Jew or a hunter in a Persian frieze.

Bill revives the Hardwar joke about who will share a room with whom—there seem to be only a couple of rooms available in the guest house for the night—and the conversation becomes a little giddy.

"Chacha, you can sleep with Cran Sahib and Cran Memsahib," Bill says, puffing at his pipe.

Chachaji registers no emotion. He simply says, "That would not be convenient."

Bill becomes flushed with laughter.

"Cran Sahib has the shining-red face of a gentleman," Chachaji observes.

Then everyone laughs.

"But who is going to share a room with Eoin?" Bill asks. "His snoring is reputed to keep camels awake."

"Snoring is one of my greatest pleasures," Eoin says, without any self-consciousness.

"I've often shared a room with Eoin," Ivan says. "And I can say one thing: whatever I lost in sleep at night was made up for by the good cheer of his company during the day."

A bearer comes in and says that a third room is available, and the subject of sharing rooms is dropped for the moment. Chachaji soon falls asleep in a corner, with a Buddhalike expression, and is forgotten.

"I wonder what really happens in a storm like this to people who live in mud huts," Jane says.

"If they can't find shelter under a tin roof or in a brick house, they can be killed by the hailstones," I say. "Fortunately, such severe storms are rare."

Bill now grows excited. He seizes on the storm as a chance for a great journalistic coup. "We must go back to the village tomorrow and film the effects of the storm," he says. "Maybe we will be able to show some dead cattle, some destroyed houses. The storm is the best thing that's happened to our film. It may be a whole film in itself." He is at his journalistic best, seeing new significance in Ivan's earlier rain shots and random village shots as he plots new storm shots. "Look, we have shots of sun over the village, gray sky over the village, specks of rain in the village, darkness over the village—and now we have, from Bahani, big storm clouds, lightning in the night, and a hailstorm in what could all be the village. We also have shots of bullock carts trotting along in water and of people running into their houses. We'll be able to give the impression that they are running for shelter from the storm. If we go back and do some more shooting, we'll be able to show what devastation the storm brought to the village."

"Maybe the storm passed the village by completely," I say.

"God, what an awful thought!" Bill says.

"I don't know how people have managed to survive here at all," Ivan says. "I think what they really need is a full-scale Communist revolution."

"Ivan, have you read any Solzhenitsyn?" Bill asks mischievously.

"He is a reactionary turncoat," Ivan says. "Sometimes awful things have to be done to bring about a better society."

"Hitler also said that," Bill says. "How do you feel about Hitler?"

Ivan becomes agitated almost to the point of speechlessness. Most of the time, he is the passionate provocateur, turning an opponent's remarks on their head in the proverbial Marxist manner. We call him "the moving target," because it is impossible to fix a sight on him.

Bill, who has an infallible eye for people's weak points, goes after Ivan's Marxism. "Stalin was as bad as Hitler," he says. "Purges in Russia can no more be justified than extermination camps in Germany."

Ivan tries to fight him off. "Drawing such comparisons is the last refuge of a capitalist imperialist."

The remark would be funny if it weren't for the bitter tone, since Bill often acts like an old-fashioned British Army major. Even when there is no call to lead anyone anywhere, he takes the role of a leader at the head of his troops. "Suppose the Germans had not attacked the Soviet Union and had won the Second World War," he says now. "In that case, would the Germans have been right in thinking that Hitler's atrocities were justified because they had led to such great gains?"

For once, Bill had turned Ivan's argument on its head. Ivan tries to regain his balance. "The oldest trick in the book is to confuse revolutionary purge with genocide."

The remark sounds flat, and Jane, whom Ivan always protects, as if her position as his assistant were a testing ground for his Marxist beliefs, tries to help him out by defending Trotsky at the expense of Stalin, but she succeeds only in muddying the waters.

Bill presses his attack, almost going beyond the bounds of good taste. "Ivan, your political views are emotional," he says, with a laugh. "They must come from your Communist mother."

Ivan stammers.

Eoin abruptly changes the subject—clearly trying to ease the tension. "I fought something of a world war with bedbugs in Kabul, and they really fought dirty," he says.

Chachaji wakes up. "Cran Sahib, what time is it?" he asks. "Can I have tea and buttered toast?"

"Tea and buttered toast for Chacha and more whiskey for the rest of us!" Bill cries.

There is no more whiskey to be had. The bearer, however, produces some Indian beer. Ivan insists that the bearer, the cook, and the drivers all sit down with us and drink beer. Yoginder Singh takes great delight in joining the circle. He draws up a big armchair and puts his feet on the table. The other servants retreat behind the window curtains with their glasses of beer, having taken the precaution of locking the drawing-room doors, so the other guests will not surprise them and think they are taking liberties.

When we finally decide to go to bed, Chachaji refuses our offer to share any of the three available rooms. (We later learn that he went off with the drivers, and the three of them slept in the servants' quarters, on a single bed, under one blanket—beds and bedclothes being as scarce as rooms that night.)

March 3rd

E VERYONE EXCEPT, PERHAPS, CHACHAJI HAS SLEPT well. Bill seems as eager to be off to the village as if he were a cub reporter, but Ivan, Eoin, and Jane linger over their coffee even more than usual, apparently reluctant to face the possible devastation of the village.

Bill hustles them along. "I can't wait to go and see what toll the storm has taken in the village. Maybe the whole village was wiped out. Maybe Chacha's relatives have been ruined. The destruction of the village will help me to underline the point that the villagers' lives are precarious—that Chacha's life is precarious. Maybe the storm's devastation is such that we can build the whole film around it."

It's clear that a vision of major disaster is dancing in Bill's head, but the others seem pained and skeptical.

Chachaji, catching the drift of Bill's remarks, is worried. "The talk of Cran Sahib may bring bad luck," he says.

As soon as we reach Amanpur and get out of the cars, Om Prakash and a small crowd of villagers come running to greet us.

"What happened last night?" Bill asks. "Anyone die?"

"No one died," Om Prakash says.

"God has spared us," the crowd murmurs.

It seems that the hailstones in the village were much smaller than those that fell on Bahani and Karnal. Moreover, the crops, being still young, were mostly too close to the ground to be flattened by hail. Then, too, the storm came up slowly here, giving the villagers time to take precautions, such as moving their cattle inside their huts.

"But we hear that some people and many cows and bullocks were pelted to death in the villages a few miles down the road," Om Prakash says.

"Damn," Bill says. "Just our luck to have a village that escaped the storm." But he is quick to rally. "Of course, it doesn't change the fact that these villagers lead a really precarious existence."

Bill fires off a series of questions about the storm. Various people answer, sometimes speaking at once.

"What would have happened if the storm had destroyed all your crops?" he asks.

"We would have had to borrow from one another and somehow pull through."

"How often do you get a really bad storm around here?"

"Every two or three years. But this is the second storm this year—something that has never happened before in our memory."

"When you get a really bad storm, does that mean you have nothing to sell that year?"

"No. We plant twice a year, so even if one crop is ruined, we can still look forward to the second to save us."

Bill is seeking desperate, cataclysmic revelations,

but the villagers reply calmly and matter-of-factly. Bill turns on me in frustration. "Are you translating correctly? You aren't editing their answers, are you?"

I tell him that I am not leaving anything out, and explain that here in the Punjab the effects of a storm are not as devastating as they are in other parts of India, because the Punjab is a more prosperous region to begin with and its people are more resilient. I go on to reassure him that the kind of storm sequence he had in mind was, however, true to the spirit, if not to the letter, of what can and does happen to an Indian village.

We all walk down to the village, which looks much as it did yesterday—poor and quiet. Ivan takes some shots of vultures circling over wet trees; of a bullock cart—overflowing with hay—mired in a field, with some vacant-looking hay cutters struggling together to push it loose; of another bullock cart splashing through an overflowing stream and getting stuck in it; of flattened crops; of some villagers trudging through knee-deep water. These are actually shots that we could have taken after any ordinary rain, but Bill says, "I can cut them together with all the other shots we have, and make a really horrific storm sequence."

For me, the boon of the storm is that it has given us a second chance at the village, and we can now take the shots we missed of Chachaji with the shopkeepers and with the swami. As it happens, we are able to film a very effective sequence with the shopkeepers, who, as soon as they spot Chachaji, spontaneously leave their shops and greet him, as if he were a man of substance.

"Did you have this wretched tie on yesterday?"

Bill suddenly asks Chachaji, having noticed that Chachaji is wearing an old plain-blue nylon necktie.

Chachaji cannot remember, and neither can anyone else.

"We can't show him in the village sometimes with a tie and sometimes without a tie," Bill says. "It's going to present me with one hell of a continuity problem." Then he says, with a laugh, "Sally, from now on, keep on the lookout for any changes in Chacha's haberdashery."

In search of the swami, we go to the village temple, which is a simple structure set on a knoll by a little lake. Bill positions Chachaji a few yards away from the temple. Yoginder Singh and Amarjit Singh hold back the shopkeepers, children, and other people who are following us. We begin filming. Chachaji walks into the open courtyard in front of the temple. To our delight, just at the moment—as if on cue—an ancient, toothless man with a long white beard comes out of the temple. He is the swami. Like Chachaji, he is wearing a turban, but his turban is ivory—less striking than Chachaji's. The two men greet each other in the Indian manner—bringing the palms of their hands together and bowing slightly.

Ivan keeps the camera rolling to see what will happen next, but both men seem suddenly confused and stare into the camera. Ivan cuts.

Chachaji and the swami sit down on the bare ground by a tree. In the strong daylight, they both look very old and very weatherbeaten—rather like a pair of ancient mariners. Bill is disappointed, almost sullen; he had hoped that the two old men would offer a strong visual contrast, whereas in fact they look very much alike, except that Chachaji doesn't have a beard. Then Bill cheers up, for the swami, in a spontaneous gesture, unwinds a layer or two of his turban and throws it around his neck like a scarf, in the manner of some holy men.

Next, without any prompting, the swami begins singing a complicated Sanskrit prayer. It is one of the few Sanskrit prayers that Chachaji doesn't know, so all he can do is to mumble after the swami. Suddenly, the swami pauses, as if he had lost the thread, and Chachaji boldly takes the lead and starts singing his own prayer. It is now the swami's turn to mumble after Chachaji. Chachaji is radiant. He knows almost two hundred prayers by heart, and now he has an opportunity to shine before the swami he reveres.

"It's an immortal scene," Bill says with glee.

Bill wants to go on shooting Chachaji with the swami, but Jane tells him we are on the last roll of film. Bill brought only ten rolls from Delhi, thinking that the village could not possibly yield much more than twice the Hardwar material, which had used up four rolls.

Eoin has plenty of tapes—compared to the bulky rolls of film, the tapes take up practically no space—and he records Chachaji and the swami singing hymns together: first the swami leading and Chachaji following, then the other way around.

When the singing is over, Chachaji comes up to me and asks in a whisper, "Could I have a note or two to give to the swamiji?"

I give him a ten-rupee note. Chachaji walks up to

The Swami and Chachaji Chanting

the swami with the note in his hand and ceremoniously presents it to him. The swami accepts the money and blesses him. There is something very touching about this scene—a poor old man who looks as if he could scarcely meet his own needs giving money to another poor old man.

Bill watches rather sadly. "That was a really nice spontaneous gesture," Bill says. "Really moving. I wish I'd brought just one more roll. But I have to husband what's left in the camera, in case we can get some shots of storm devastation on the way back to Delhi."

When we return to the cars, practically the entire village comes to say goodbye: the women relatives who laughed at our fumbling with the fresh eggs; the shopkeepers; the hay cutters; the schoolchildren. All the villagers appear sorry to see us go, but Chachaji's old sister-in-law seems really grieved, as if she feared that she might not live to see Chachaji again.

English Singh consoles her. "But I am here," he says. "I can speak English."

As we drive away, Bill—back in the Ambassador with us—says, "The peace and quiet of the swami scene will make a marvellous end to the village sequence, especially if we make a sharp cut from there to the noise and horribleness of Delhi." He becomes so engrossed in how he will edit the film that he pays little attention to the countryside we are passing through.

Suddenly, Sally cries out, "Look at that!" She shudders.

Yoginder Singh brakes the car, and we all get out. Some distance off the road, in a patch of mire, dozens of vultures are fighting over the half-buried carcass of a cow. We creep along the road so as not to startle them, but the precaution is unnecessary; they are bold and shameless, and it seems that they will allow nothing to interfere with their ghoulish business. Some of the vultures sit on a high stone wall near the carcass, their fat, ungainly bodies almost inert. Now and again, a whole gang of them swoops down on the half-eaten carcass, and they vie over choice bits of meat. Others circle around wailing and screaming, making an eerie cacophony in the quiet of the road. A wild-looking dog, his head and muzzle dripping with the cow's blood, gnaws intently at one end of the carcass.

"This is great!" Bill says. "It can be used as a dramatic illustration of the real devastation of the storm."

"The cow could have died several days ago, before the storm," I say.

"It certainly looks that way," Sally says.

"On film, it'll look freshly dead," Bill says.

From the roadside, Ivan takes a long shot, but he complains that because the vultures are so thickly clustered it won't be clear exactly what they are doing.

Bill takes a stone and throws it at the horde. The stone falls in their midst, but they scarcely twitch. "God! They are really single-minded," he says. "I don't think one of them will leave until they have finished the last bit of meat."

"I think I'd better go over to the other side and take a closeup of the carcass," Ivan says.

I warn Ivan that the dog could be rabid, but he is so caught up in getting a good shot that his own safety seems to be his last concern. With Eoin and Jane following, Ivan creeps away toward the other side of the carcass. However, he is not able to take a single shot of the vultures. The moment they catch sight of the camera, they fly away. Perhaps the shine of its gunlike metal frightened them.

March 4th

B ACK IN DELHI, I HOLD OUT TO BILL, AT THE breakfast table, a morning newspaper with a prominent story about the hailstorm. He is busy putting marmalade on his toast, and Araminta takes the paper.

"One person was killed and nine were injured in the storm," Araminta reads out in her strong, stagy English voice. "Hundreds of cattle perished and crops in about twenty villages were damaged. . . . Most villages hit by the hailstorm had been affected by floods last year. . . . The ruins of the hutments and roofs blown off by the storm and large holes caused in the roofs of houses made of corrugated sheets are indications of the severity of the hailstorm, which, according to the octogenarian Mr. Usman Khan of Kherla (near Nuh), was the worst ever in living memory. . . . All along the three km. route between Nuh and Muradhas village this reporter saw carcasses of animals and birds killed in the squall. Barely a few trees were left with some leaves and stalks intact. The lush green fields of golden wheat and yellow sarson are in ruins."

"It's our damn bad luck that Amanpur wasn't hit

this way," Bill says. "But, frankly, I don't know if our going to the village at all was worth the effort."

This remark surprises me, although by now I should know better than to be surprised by anything Bill says. He has a way of getting very excited while we are planning sequences or taking shots—throwing himself into the work with energy and enthusiasm, and going to almost any lengths to get a good shot. If at the time those sequences and shots go well, he will exult, and ask everyone to join in his exultation, like a child. But later on he will talk about the same sequences and shots as if they were just wasted time and effort. I reflect that these changes of mood may stem from a capricious nature, or from a fear that if he doesn't continually prod us to work harder and keep searching for better material we will slack off, or from the natural anxiety of someone who bears ultimate responsibility for a creative effort over which he actually has little control.

Chachaji is unavailable this morning, because he has to go to the tax office to obtain the forms for Chopra that are available only on this particular Saturday. So we decide to look up Tara Chachi. I learned from Madan and his wife during one of Chachaji's visits to them that Tara Chachi lives with Avtar Singh, in the compound of a center for teaching the indigenous system of Unani medicine, in a pleasant residential area called Karol Bagh. They occupy one of the dwellings that make up the servants' quarters—rows and rows of mustard-colored plaster-faced structures, two or three stories high.

In the front yard of Tara Chachi's house are some

bushes and a clothesline, on which worn articles of women's underwear are flapping mournfully in the breeze. An elderly Sikh and a sour-looking woman are sitting on a jute-string cot on the veranda. I presume that the woman must be Tara Chachi, although she bears no resemblance to the saucy young woman of my childhood.

I approach the veranda with Bill and Sally, and speak to the Sikh, saying what Madan's wife had told me to say: that I live in Manhattan, which is near Bayside, Queens, where one of Avtar Singh's (or Chachaji's) daughters is now settled. The Sikh immediately takes Bill, Sally, and me into the house with him. The woman, who is never introduced, stays where she is.

Inside, a number of children, young men, and young women are lounging around on cots and chairs, and there is very little space to move about. Sally and I manage to sit down at the foot of a cot, and Bill slumps into a chair and closes his eyes. He opens them for a moment, as a way of displaying his annoyance at not knowing who is who in the room. The Sikh makes no attempt to introduce anyone.

I elicit from the Sikh the fact that he is indeed Avtar Singh.

"Aha! The lodger!" Bill exclaims. "Is that woman outside Chacha's wife?"

I put the question to Avtar Singh.

"She is Bahali Ram's ex-wife," the Sikh says. "But what's the use of stirring up old coals?"

I ask Avtar Singh what he does for a livelihood.

"I don't work," he says. "Every time I have worked, it has come to no good."

"How do you manage to make ends meet, then?" I ask.

"Before Partition, I had a lot of land. Now I live on the interest on loans I make. I also own two scooter-rickshaws, which I rent out."

When I translate this, Bill sits up. "It would be just like Chacha to have an old layabout run away with his wife."

"There's very little light here for shooting," Ivan says, poking his head around the door. "Besides, what is there to shoot here, anyway?"

Bill gets up briskly and says, "Right. Let's get the old layabout and the wife to do something."

I ask Avtar Singh how Tara Chachi spends her day.

"She is not well—she has just had a heart attack," he says.

"Then let's set up the old layabout in the front yard, scolding a scooter-wallah for not paying his daily rent on time," Bill says. "Chacha's runaway wife can stay put on the bed in front, then slowly shuffle off and stretch out just inside, on this bed. I think she's up to that much, isn't she? It'll just about make a sequence that we can flash to when you say in your commentary, 'Poor old Chacha once had a wife, but the wife ran away with a layabout.' "

"I'll write my own commentary, thank you," I tell Bill.

He laughs.

March 5th

"**L**ET'S GET YOUR FATHER'S DAILY WALK AROUND Humayun's tomb on film," Bill says at breakfast. "He is the most photogenic member of your family, and his walk around the Moghul tomb will really give us some contrast to old Chacha's shuffle through the dirty bazaars."

Although it is ten o'clock—three hours later than the normal time for Daddyji's walk—we pick him up at the house and drive him to Humayun's tomb, a series of formal walled gardens with arches and terraces, dominated by the mausoleum of the Moghul emperor and dotted with smaller tombs. We find the garden overrun by foreign tourists.

"The last thing we want to show is Germans, Swedes, and Danes moghuling it up in India," Bill says.

Eventually, we come upon an inner garden that is practically deserted. It has a small tomb of its own, which looks impressive enough.

"Let's have Daddyji walk down the path, up the steps, and under this archway," Bill says, and we start filming.

Daddyji, who is a little bit of a ham, jauntily places his walking stick across his shoulders as he reaches the steps.

Bill is delighted. "That's lovely—it's so raj. He's got something of Olivier in him."

March 6th

B ILL COMES TO MY ROOM AROUND TEN, WITH
notebook and pencil in hand and Araminta
in tow. "I've given the crew the day off, so
that we can have a brainstorming session," he
says. "Frankly, I've never been so unhappy in
my life. I don't know if it is a product of my
nerves, or what, but our situation, as I see it, is really
grim. Our film is repetitive. There's no progression. It
goes round and round in circles. It has no conflict, no
dramatic tension, no story line. I think we'll be lucky
if we can come up with twenty minutes of usable
film—which is about the natural length for a film on
Chacha. Nothing is sadder than to have a film whose
natural length is twenty or thirty minutes stretched
out. That's the surest way to run a film into the ground.
And remember, I have a fifty-seven-minute hole in the
air to fill—no more, no less. A thirty- or forty- or fifty-
minute film is just as useless as no film at all."

I reflect that ever since we began shooting, Bill has
been complaining that we don't have enough usable
material. As he gets more new material, the old material recedes in his memory, and he ruthlessly dispar-
ages it, with the result that the length he projects for
sequences—and hence for the film—keeps shrinking.
One day, Chachaji's bus sequence is good for thirty-
five seconds; the next day, for only eighteen seconds;

the day after that, for ten seconds; and finally it's worthless—unusable.

I know from my own experience that anxiety is an inescapable part of working on long projects, and I continually try to reassure him. But now I ask him, "How can you tell how long a film you will have until you screen the rushes?"

"Because I've had eight years of television experience," he says. "That's how."

Araminta says, "I think one question you haven't faced, Ved—and it's a question that goes to the heart of the problem with the film—is, Why Chacha? You have a personal interest in him, but no one else has. Even the crew think a film on Chacha is boring. The millions of people who will see Bill's film don't know you and have no reason to care about you or Chacha. I just don't think there is a story to be told. But it's for you and Bill to sort out. I'm leaving." She gets up and goes out.

"Let's clear the decks," Bill says. "I really don't think there's any more meat on Chacha's bones. As I said, we just might have enough material for a short— say, twenty minutes. Then we have to make another short, on a different subject, to run back to back with it. What I would like best is to forget about Chacha and make a whole new fifty-seven-minute film. We still have enough time and stock to start over."

I am horrified. "The idea of a whole new film at this stage is preposterous," I tell him. "I think that our best hope is to stay with the Chacha story and explore it to its limits."

"But I have to think about those millions of viewers," Bill says.

"Worrying about millions of viewers is a mistake," I say. "Since you can never really know what they want, trying to please them is a good way to paralyze yourself. We should think of ourselves as the ideal viewers and make a film that pleases us. If we succeed in pleasing ourselves, the chances are we will please others."

"It sounds good, but it's unrealistic," Bill says. "Besides, it's not just a matter of pleasing the viewers but of telling them as much as we possibly can about India in fifty-seven minutes. Our film may be the only thing many American viewers will ever see on the country."

"I was born and brought up in India. I've been writing about India for years. Yet I feel I have hardly scratched the surface. And here you are wanting to convey India in less than an hour. It's a dream."

We talk in this vein for some time and get nowhere. Then I ask Bill, "Can you sum up the core of your objection to the Chacha film?"

"He's simply too fortunate a man in India," Bill says. "He has a roof over his head. He has plumbing. He has a job. He has a family to look after him. Nothing about him suggests the abyss. We have to find a way of conveying the full power and scope of Indian poverty—of that abyss."

"People in the West know about Indian poverty, but they run away from it, because they feel they can do nothing about it—it remains an abstraction to them.

One reason for choosing Chachaji in the first place was that people in the West could identify with his problems in a way they couldn't with the problems of the really destitute. I wanted to get inside the problem of poverty—to involve people in it. I wanted to show how the poor survive—how one man survives."

"It's just not working."

As a last gambit, I suggest demonstrating how fortunate Chachaji is by intercutting his day with shots of people much less fortunate. "First, we could show Chachaji in his room, waking up. Then we could show people waking up in the streets. We could show Chachaji washing at a sink and then cut to people washing in an open drain. We could show Chachaji walking, vigorously waving his arms and pushing his way through a crowd, and then cut to sick, deformed people being pushed aside by the crowd. We could show Chachaji in a family setting and then cut to slum hostelries where row upon row of homeless men sleep on stone floors. I should say that I myself am lukewarm about the idea, because it's bound to diffuse Chachaji's story and to seem crude, but perhaps it will give you greater scope."

"That's what I've been waiting to hear for three bloody weeks!" Bill cries, his whole demeanor changing. "It will give the film that extra dimension that it cries out for. If I have that kind of material, then I can make the Chacha story work for fifty-seven minutes—show him teetering on the brink of the abyss. Where can we get shots of the abyss quickly?"

"We can get them right here in Delhi."

"But Delhi is so boring," Bill says. "And, remember, if the device is to work we need really shocking, horrific shots."

"If you want pictures of the worst poverty you can imagine, then I suppose we could go to Bombay or Calcutta. There you can walk out of a hotel in the best section of the city and see people sleeping, defecating, washing, living, and dying in the streets. The trouble is that in those cities we would be getting shots not of Punjabis but of Maharashtrians or Bengalis."

"Hell, no Westerner can tell a Punjabi from a Bengali. I don't care who they are, as long as we get the abyss. Wouldn't Calcutta be the best place for it?"

"There comes a point in degradation where distinctions between poor and poorer are meaningless. But certainly there's nothing in the world comparable to the poverty visible in Calcutta."

"Visually, Calcutta will be great," Bill says, running away with the idea.

"This intercutting business has to be handled very delicately, if we use it at all," I say, trying to restrain him. "Otherwise, it will turn a simple story—a window on India—into a melodramatic extravaganza."

"I'm not worried about that. Could we, for instance, find a village that is much poorer than Chacha's and do a one-for-one correlation of his story with the abyss?"

"Sure, there are villages much poorer than Chachaji's. But if the device is used mechanically—"

"Hell, I wouldn't use the device mechanically. I just need the shots."

I realize that the integrity of the film will now depend more than ever on Bill's judgment in the editing room. If it turns out that we get enough material for a full-length film on Chachaji, Bill may refrain from using the horrific images of poverty; but if it turns out that he does have to use those images, I can only trust that he will exercise a certain amount of restraint. What I privately hope is that two or three days' filming in Calcutta will calm Bill's nerves and then we can resume work on Chachaji.

To my surprise, Bill says, "Let's go to Calcutta tomorrow." He sounds happier than he has sounded in days.

"The day after tomorrow," I say. "I'll need a day to make the necessary arrangements. Also, I should warn you that filming in Calcutta will present us with some very special problems. The authorities there are so sensitive about the image of their city that they will let us film only things that show Calcutta in a good light. The people themselves are so sensitive about their poverty, and so volatile, that we may need a police escort to film there at all. And, even with a police escort, we could have a riot on our hands if we are not careful. Calcutta is notorious for its mob violence."

"It sounds exciting," Bill says. "I've filmed in war zones, and I think I can handle Calcutta."

"Another thing. I won't be of very much use to you in Calcutta, because I don't speak any Bengali, and the Bengalis are so chauvinistic about their language and culture that most of them don't bother to learn any other language. I will be just as much a foreigner there as you and everyone else in the team. I wonder what would have happened to us in Hardwar if I had not been able to speak to the crowd in Hindi."

"There are always ways to wing it," he says. "We can charm the authorities, or, if worst comes to worst, we can film from the car."

March 7th

"THIS HOLE IS DAMN NEAR PERFECT," BILL SAYS. "It's really powerfully squalid."

We are crammed into Chachaji's favorite teashop, where he often refreshes himself between errands. It is a close little one-room affair whose walls and ceiling are dripping with grease, and its proprietor is a fat, pugnacious, loud man with a handlebar mustache. Yoginder Singh and Amarjit Singh somehow manage to hold back the inevitable crowd that materializes at the entrance.

Jane claps the board, and the proprietor starts playing up to the camera.

"I will serve the star sahib myself!" he shouts to the cook, who is working at a clay oven in the back of the room.

The people crowding around the entrance laugh.

"He is spoiling the shot," Bill tells me. "Tell him not to make any special fuss over Chacha."

But there is no controlling the histrionic proprietor. He presses patties and tea on Chachaji, and continually bellows and gesticulates.

Bill signals to Ivan to cut.

"This place is not fit for a photograph," Chachaji says, in his usual quiet manner. "The proprietor is not a gentleman. He is a trouble-producer."

Everyone laughs, but we leave quickly.

ONE OF THE ERRANDS that Chachaji regularly does for the chemist is to take some samples of chemicals to a government laboratory and get them tested and certified. We have filmed the chemist giving him the samples, but we have not filmed Chachaji delivering them, so today we go with Chachaji to the laboratory, which is in a bleak factory area of severe-looking buildings, demolition sites, piles of rubble, and empty lots, and, oddly, is housed in a soap-and-chemical factory. We film him first making his way past emaciated men stirring large vats of soap at the front of the building, and then delivering a sample to a laboratory assistant—who turns out to be one of the few people who treat Chachaji with a certain amount of natural courtesy. Then, with Chachaji, we go to the Intercontinental Hotel for lunch.

Chachaji has never walked into a big Western-style hotel before, and the Intercontinental has Western amenities of all kinds—central air-conditioning, elevators, Western-type shops, hairdressers, a swimming pool.

"What do you think of this place?" I ask him.

"It's quite all right," he says.

I am taken aback until I remember that he scarcely notices what conditions he lives in, what conditions he works in, where he is sent, or how he gets there. It is as though in order to survive and function he couldn't afford to notice very much or to react much to anything—as though he had had to anesthetize himself to practically everything.

But then he beckons to me and exclaims, "Five rupees for a cup of tea!" Money is the one thing to which he is not anesthetized. "I'd have trouble swallowing it. It costs less than a rupee in my favorite teashop. What can be so special about this tea?"

"What's he saying?" Bill asks. "Tell the old sod to enjoy himself while he can. He's only a superstar while we are here."

"That bicycle-drawn rickshaw I saw out there didn't suggest anything intercontinental to me," Ivan remarks.

"Does Chacha ever ride in a bicycle-rickshaw?" Bill asks, immediately getting serious.

"Sure," I say. "He doesn't take buses except to go long distances."

"It would be lovely to see him in one of those contraptions," Bill says. "It would be terrific to show him barrelling through the most congested bazaar in a wobbly old bicycle-rickshaw. Do those things ever turn over?"

"They can have very bad accidents," I say.

"What's one of the most congested, colorful bazaars?" Bill asks.

"Chandni Chowk," I tell him, adding, "It is near the State Bank, where we have already shown him doing an errand."

Bill insists that we drive to Chandni Chowk the moment we finish lunch.

On the way to Chandni Chowk, we pass by the Secretariat, one of the most imposing government buildings in New Delhi, which dates from British times. Bill stops the cars and calls for a shot of "Chacha as a human ant crawling in the shadow of the high and mighty."

"What will Bill think of next?" Ivan says as he finishes the shot. "You watch! He'll have Chacha climbing up the Secretariat wall."

In the Chandni Chowk area, Bill selects the most decrepit-looking bicycle-rickshaw he can find—with the most pathetic-looking coolie—and asks Chachaji to get in.

Chachaji balks. Left to himself, he would choose the sturdiest-looking bicycle-rickshaw. Bill practically lifts him into the bicycle-rickshaw and then loads it with a couple of sacks of flour he borrows from a roadside vender, to make the contraption look even more dangerously unsteady than it actually is. He directs the coolie to follow the station wagon, and we set off, with the Ambassador, this once, in the rear.

It is about five o'clock in the afternoon, and Chandni Chowk—the busiest thoroughfare in Old Delhi, always crowded and disorderly—is now jammed with pedestrians, cows, tongas, cars, bicycles, motorcycles, scooters, scooter-rickshaws, coolie-rickshaws, bicycle-rickshaws, handcarts. There is a general din of klaxons, hooters, bicycle bells, cowbells, hawkers' cries, coolies' imprecations. Everyone seems to be trapped in the chaotic thoroughfare, and seems to be trying to run down everyone else in order to get out of it.

From the back of the station wagon, Ivan films Chachaji's bicycle-rickshaw weaving its way through the melee of vehicles, pedestrians, and animals. But then the traffic gets so thick that we can't move. Ivan gets into the bicycle-rickshaw with Chachaji to do some tracking shots.

"Sahib, my legs won't pull the weight," the coolie cries. "Sahib, the rickshaw will overturn."

Bill hands the coolie a ten-rupee note.

"Cran Sahib, I beg to get out!" Chachaji cries, waving his arms and trying to scramble out.

"Just hang in there a few more minutes," Bill says. "You make a terrific photograph."

"Let it be," Chachaji says, shrinking into the corner of the rickshaw carriage, frightened and resigned.

Together, Ivan and Chachaji disappear in the crowd.

"We'll show him in this rickshaw during the bank and tax-office sequences," Bill says to me as we wait in the car. "He'll look so intimidated by it all that people's sympathy will be immediately engaged."

WE CATCH THE 7 A.M. AIRBUS to Calcutta and check into the Grand Hotel, which was once regarded as the modern wonder of Asia but is now something of an embarrassment amid the poverty of Calcutta. Even before we settle in, Bill comes to me and asks, "Where is the abyss?"

"It's all around you," I say. "You saw it, coming from the airport."

"But I mean the *real* abyss. Something that'll jump off the screen and grab you. I want pictures that may be on the screen no more than twenty or thirty seconds but will shout 'Indian poverty!'"

I feel sure that if we were prepared to spend a week making the rounds of state offices we could obtain permission from the local authorities to take the kind of shots Bill wants, and even get a police escort. But since we can afford only three days in Calcutta, I decide that we should try to shoot without permission. I warn Bill and all the others that it's very risky, and make them promise that the minute I decide it's dangerous we'll stop, even if we are in the middle of shooting.

I finally find a couple of more or less reliable-looking taxi-drivers with a smattering of English or Hindi who have more or less reliable-looking cars, and hire them to take us around for a couple of days. We set off for Howrah, which lies across the Hooghly River from Calcutta proper, and which is one of the poorest townships in the metropolis.

On the way, we stop at the Howrah Bridge, under which live people who are little more than skin and bones.

In Howrah itself, we find deformed beggars crawling around the railway station.

"I have better shots of poverty in the village," Bill says.

Next, I take the team to the city's cremation ground, where the air is thick with flying ash. The cremation ground is a walled-in stretch of desolate riverbank open to the sky and given over to rows of burning pyres and small crowds of gaunt mourners. Shrieking vultures hover overhead. They swoop down and glide menacingly past the pyres. A solitary palm tree waves in the hot, ash-laden air.

"This is what I've been looking for," Bill tells me. Then he says, gloomily, "But it's worth only a few seconds of film."

An attendant, however, informs us that all filming at the "holy place" is strictly forbidden.

"What about sneaking a shot?" Bill asks.

"We'll have a religious riot on our hands and be lucky to get away unhurt," I say.

Bill is angry. "I wish I had never seen this place," he says. "To be here and not to be able to film—that beats everything."

I pacify him by saying that perhaps we can apply to higher-ups for permission to film in the cremation ground after we've got all the other shots we want.

I take the team to a colony of Untouchables living in a muddy little back lane near another bridge. As we walk down the lane, a cow is being slaughtered and gutted. The able-bodied, women, children, the old—all are employed in washing, drying, and treating hides, using a few primitive machines, which whir and clack in the dead air. The whole place has the stench of people and animals living close together, and of rot and death.

"Jesus! If people knew what went into making those Indian sandals they buy in Harvard Square, I wonder if they would go near them," Bill says.

"At least, they give people work," Araminta says.

Bill tells Ivan and Eoin to get the equipment out of the cars, but just then a couple of wild-looking dogs start toward us. I warn everyone that the dogs may be rabid, and we run back to the cars.

"It's too dark for shooting now anyway," Bill says. "We'll have to come back in daylight."

March 9th

"WHAT HAVE YOU COME ACROSS HERE IN YOUR PREvious visits that you remember as being really ——— horrible?" Bills asks.

I tell him about Dhapa dump, where all the refuse and filth of Calcutta proper are deposited, and where a whole tribe of people lives by scavenging.

"Let's have a crack at that first," Bill says. "We can go back to the Untouchable colony later."

Before we have driven even a couple of hundred yards—almost in the back yard of the hotel—we come upon a familiar morning sight in Calcutta: people defecating in the street, and city sweepers, bent over short-handled shovels, sweeping up the ordure and piling it on a city lorry bound for the dump.

As we get out to take a shot of the sweepers and the lorry, to introduce the dump sequence, the driver says to me nervously, "This is not a good place for filming, Sahib. A while ago, a crowd beat up an American television man and set his car on fire on this very spot."

I say that we should all get back into the taxis, and tell Ivan to shoot from the safety of his taxi. He calls back to me, "I have insurance. If anything happens to me here and I can't work, I can go back to London, sit home with my wife, and collect a hundred pounds a week. Bill has the same insurance."

All the same, we scramble into the taxis, and Ivan shoots quickly from his window; we drive off before we have attracted much attention.

"That was useless," Bill says. "What we need for a really horrific shot is a closeup of the shovels." He keeps his eyes fixed intently on the people in the streets, as if he might be able to will a shot into existence. "Stop!" he cries suddenly, almost leaping out of the moving car. Ahead, twenty or thirty emaciated men are crowded around an extraordinary scaffolding supporting a primitive assembly of ropes and pulleys and a huge weight, like the head of a mallet, which the men are using to drive a piling into the bank of a stream—probably for a footbridge. First one lot of men, then another, with almost clockwork regularity, throw themselves at the ropes, pull and heave, in a struggle to get the weight up high over their heads, and fall back as it comes crashing down and strikes the piling. The physical exertion is so relentless and the men are so feeble that to keep their spirits up and keep the rhythm of their work going they chant fragments of a work song between the dead sounds of the weight striking the piling. The scaffolding, the movements of heads and arms, the ropes, the weight make a tableau reminiscent of ancient slavery. The scene bespeaks limitless cheap labor, limitless drudgery, limitless time—

Men Driving Piles

something that could be seen only in an appallingly poor city, where men and women would mortgage their souls to get a day's work and a piece of bread at the end of it.

"This is what Calcutta is about," Bill says.

"I don't know where you'll use it," I say.

"That doesn't matter. I want it."

I talk to the drivers, and conclude that since we are away from the main thoroughfares it is safe to film. We all get out, and Ivan takes closeups of heads bent in concentration, of arms pulling and straining at the ropes, of ropes coiling limply into heaps on the ground, of ropes flying as the men let go. Eoin records the gasping and chanting of the men, and the goading cries of a foreman to get them to sing louder and work harder. Their work song sounds increasingly like the prayers of condemned prisoners.

We drive on.

The air at Dhapa is gritty and alive with flying insects. Our hands and faces and clothes are almost at once covered with grit. Overhead, vultures fight, shrieking as if the dump were another cremation ground. The dump seems eerily deserted. City lorries sporadically pull up and unload the collected filth of Calcutta streets—mostly excrement. In the distance, an old bulldozer is levelling hills of filth.

We all get out of the cars. My driver immediately begins complaining, "Sahib, this is a place of sickness and disease. If I get sick here today, how will I earn my daily wage? Who will look after my wife and children? We should not stay here."

I tell him that we will stay only a few minutes. I

am afraid of catching some disease myself, but I am nevertheless excited.

Bill is galvanized into activity. He gets Ivan to take a shot of the bulldozer through the gritty haze, and then closeups of a lorry arriving with two sweepers in the back trying to loosen the filth with a shovel and a pick, and of another lorry backing up and disgorging its load of rubbish and ordure.

Suddenly, a dozen small, thin, monkeylike creatures with vacant faces, who could be survivors of some prehistoric age, appear from nowhere and throw themselves on top of the latest load, scavenging through it for bits of rag and scrap metal.

"What a stroke of luck!" Bill says, coming up to me. "Ivan was panning down the back of that lorry, and then, when it was fully tilted, there were all those people. He also managed to get a shot, through a tunnel of legs, of all those hands scrabbling around in the squalid heap of rubbish."

Bill and Ivan rush off up a hill for more shots, and Eoin goes in another direction to record whatever he can. The rest of us stand around coughing and trying to brush off the insects that settle on us. There is a slight breeze, which, without trees or anything else to break it, makes the place seem even emptier than before. Bill, Ivan, and Eoin are so absorbed in their work that they seem completely oblivious of personal discomfort or danger, although Bill does occasionally glance down at us for a signal of any impending trouble.

"Now we are getting somewhere," Bill says as we drive off. "That was really great. The dump is, if anything, an even stronger image than the pile-driving. It is the ultimate rock bottom."

He talks excitedly about building up a sewage sequence with the lorry shot near our hotel and the dump shots, and adds, "You'll have to help me get closeups of people waking up in the street, of people defecating in the gutter, and of the sweepers collecting the filth and loading it onto a lorry. Otherwise, the sequence won't be complete."

"I think we have already pushed our luck far enough," I say. "Taking the closeup street shots you want would start a riot. We would be jeopardizing the lives of the drivers and of all of us. We probably couldn't do it even if we had a police escort."

Bill talks bravely of having shot in Ireland during some of the worst fighting. Then he shouts "Stop!" and we halt.

At the side of the road, a couple of men are standing deep in a stream washing shirts. They send up spray as they beat the shirts repeatedly against a rock, their heads and shoulders moving up and down rhythmically, almost mechanically. They suggest the same kind of infinite toil that the pile drivers did, and we take a couple of shots of them.

"What about going back and getting some shots of the Untouchables making leather?" Bill says when we are in the car again.

I don't like the idea of going back to the colony with the stray dogs for another shot of grotesque poverty. Moreover, I can't see how such shots, good though they may be in themselves, can ever be used in a film about Chachaji. We left New York with the idea of doing a slow, delicate film about one old relative of mine, and here we are in Calcutta, many hundreds of miles away from the old relative, filming an Indian horror show.

"However carefully we use this Calcutta material, it will look sensational and melodramatic in the Chacha film," I say.

"I don't agree," Bill says. "The most beautiful films have grotesque things in them. In fact, I will go further and say that all the best things always have the worst things in them. That's what makes them the best."

"But surely writers and directors don't set out—consciously—to put the grotesque or worst things in their creations in order to make them the best," I say.

"I don't know about the grotesque, but they certainly put in the worst things," says Araminta, who is travelling in our car. "There are big hunks of many of Shakespeare's plays that are just terrible."

"But the point is, did Shakespeare consciously put them in his plays because he knew they were terrible or did he put them there because he thought they were good—and you think they are terrible?" I say.

"Of course he knew they were terrible," she says. "Take the comic bits in 'The Tempest.' They're excruciating. I'm sure Shakespeare knew they were terrible and put them in just to pander to the taste of the Elizabethan audience. No doubt they were very amusing to the Elizabethans, but we just want him to get on with the play."

"Araminta is right," Bill says. "You must always keep in mind the audience—what their tastes are. Anyway, I have a fifty-seven-minute hole in the air to fill and I've got to cover my back."

So we end up in the Untouchable colony. Bill is especially delighted when, during one shot of the leatherworkers, a train passes in the background, underscoring the squalor of the place. I am especially delighted when we leave the colony and its dogs without coming to any harm.

March 10th

A T BREAKFAST, BILL TURNS TO ME AND SAYS AS casually as if he were commenting on the weather, "Damn that Fanning. He woke me up last night, and I couldn't go back to sleep."

"What did he say?" we all cry. "Did he like the rushes?" Ever since we sent off the first shipment of film—one of several shipments—we have all been nervously waiting for some reaction to the rushes.

"I couldn't quite hear," Bill says. "There was a lot of shouting back and forth. It was a terrible connection."

"But, Bill," Araminta says, "he told you that the rushes looked smashing—that Chacha was strong enough, perhaps, to carry the whole film."

"He also said that one of the two rolls of the family dinner was completely scratched," Bill says. "And that the closeups on that roll were certainly not usable. And he said that some of the footage on the other roll of the family dinner was out of focus but that we might be able to use some of it. I can't believe that we were out of focus. And that scratch must have been a gift of GHQ's laboratory."

"What else did Fanning say?" I ask, suspecting that Bill is overplaying the bad news, just as he underplayed the good news.

"Oh, he said that all the pictures look very pretty," Bill says. "That Chacha looked stoic. But, as I said, the connection was terrible."

Despite persistent questioning, Bill refuses to say more.

March 11th

"WHAT'S ON THE AGENDA FOR THE REST OF THE day?" Eoin asks when we finish doing some early-morning shooting of people waking up, defecating, and washing in the street. While these shots are not the closeups that Bill wanted—Ivan has had to film hurriedly from the car—he thinks they will do for "the sewage sequence."

"Now that I have at least one complete abyss sequence, you chaps can take the day off," Bill says. "Our flight to Delhi is at 7 P.M."

Everyone rushes off for a swimsuit. I shout a warning not to go into the hotel pool, because no water in Calcutta is safe.

"I would really be in seventh heaven if I could just get a sequence of the cremation ground," Bill says.

"With the Hardwar shots of the Ganges, the cremation ground would be a marvellous ending to the film. That way, we could really wrap up the old boy's life— leave the viewer with an image of life and death almost superimposed on one another."

I think that ending with the cremation ground might be a little ghoulish. But Bill and I do have one thing in common—whenever we are told that we can't have something, we tend to want it more than ever and stubbornly go after it. I therefore throw myself into the task of getting the necessary permissions. I call on several ministers, commissioners, and religious leaders, and we finally do get the permissions. Bill rounds up the crew, but by this time we have only three hours left before our flight to Delhi, and the light is going fast. We decide to check out of the hotel and stop at the cremation ground on the way to the airport.

At the cremation ground, a small crowd of mourners is carrying the body of a very old man toward a pyre. A child tells me that the body is that of an old uncle who has died of a long, painful illness. I ask the mourners if we may film them. The members of the family are so grief-stricken that at first they don't understand my question, but as soon as they do they say that we may. They go ahead with their ritual as if none of us were there.

Ivan gets his camera in position and starts shooting just as the members of the family are lifting the corpse onto the pyre. He continues to film as they pile logs and sticks around the body and set a torch to the wood. The pyre burns very fast.

The last shot that Ivan takes is of the mourners standing around the pyre in the smoke, with the solitary palm tree in the background swaying slightly in the breeze. The crackling of the fire, the rustling of the palm tree, the keening of the mourners, and the shrieking of the vultures overhead mingle to give the scene of death a quality of life.

March 12th

OVER BREAKFAST IN DELHI, I SUGGEST TO BILL that we spend more time on Chachaji.

"Sure," Bill says. "Now that I have Calcutta, I'll do anything on old Chacha."

We drive to Chachaji's house. It is Sunday, and Chachaji is standing on his veranda looking forlorn.

Bill sits in the Ambassador and gazes at him for a few moments. "God, it does my heart good to see the old boy again. Who would have thought I'd miss him?"

"What are we going to shoot today?" Ivan says, walking up to our car and looking in the window at Bill. "Chacha surveying his kingdom from the veranda?"

Just then, Chachaji—tentative, as always—comes shuffling up to our cars.

"You've come," he says cryptically. "You've eaten the airs of Calcutta, Cran Sahib?"

Bill laughs.

Ved and Araminta

A stranger comes out of the house and stands on the veranda staring at us. I ask Chachaji who he is.

Chachaji has difficulty speaking. "The Arya Samaj has hired a new man to sweep and such," he says haltingly. "There is no strength in my hands and feet now for these duties. He moved in yesterday. He's a much-deserving Brahman. But it is not good for me. He is going to use all the facilities—the kitchen, the lavatory."

"So Chacha's lost his job," Bill says. "There is some meat on the Chacha bones after all. He would drop into the abyss if it weren't for your family. We finally have a story line." Bill tells the crew to get out the equipment and prepare to film Chachaji's replacement.

The members of the congregation are arriving. Daddyji, in suit and tie, appears with the president of the local branch of the Arya Samaj, a self-righteous, cantankerous old man. They are arguing.

Bill signals to Jane to put up the board quickly, and filming starts.

The president is talking loudly and unpleasantly. "You ask Bahali Ram. He can't do the work. He's too old."

Daddyji pleads with the president to keep Chachaji in his job. The president starts shouting that Bahali Ram is useless. Daddyji turns to Chachaji to get confirmation that he can do the job.

"There is no strength in my hands and feet," Chachaji says. "Sweeping is now for younger men." He clearly means it, and Daddyji looks astonished.

Daddyji changes his tack and asks the president for assurances that Chachaji will not be turned out of his room.

"I am here today," the president says. "I may not be here tomorrow. How can I give you such assurances?"

Bill cuts the shot. "The president is great," he says. "He looks really villainous. And we finally have a shot showing how Daddyji is Chacha's protector. And, to top it all off, it's spontaneous!"

On the veranda, members of the congregation are now watching a young yogi, whom they refer to as God's Celibate, strike yoga postures. The yogi has recently won a great deal of notoriety in the neighborhood because he stopped a fast-moving car by lassoing its bumper. Two deep gashes are visible on his right arm where the rope of the lasso cut into him. His feat is generally regarded here as evidence of the strength that comes from celibacy. Now the yogi contorts himself into a ball, tucking in his arms, legs, and head in such a way that he appears to have no bones—to be only a mound of flesh. In a series of odd maneuvers, he folds and whips himself into the shape of a scorpion. Chachaji watches the contortions with a completely blank expression, standing on the veranda near the door of his room. The members of the congregation, however, are mesmerized, and coo to one another about the virtues of the celibate life and the yoga postures— though they themselves are old and married and have children.

Bill gives the yogi fifty rupees to "do his act" for the camera.

Chachaji's Young Replacement

"It's one of the best mornings we've had," Bill says to me after we have finished filming. "And when I woke up this morning I had no agenda at all. It's amazing what you can sometimes get on film by sheer chance."

I remind Bill that it was the story of Chachaji's cadging razor blades from Daddyji that piqued Fanning's interest and brought us all here in the first place, and that, oddly, we haven't yet filmed that particular scene.

"Let's shoot the immortal blade scene right away," Bill says, contentedly drawing on his pipe. "It may be the crowning moment of our entire shooting. I just saw Chacha walk into your parents' house, so we will have all the facilities for a shaving sequence."

It's past ten o'clock, and Daddyji is in the bedroom. I tell him that we would like to film a shaving sequence with him and Chachaji in it. Although he has already shaved, he obligingly puts a big bath towel over his necktie and sits down in an armchair to shave a second time.

Mamaji sets down in front of Daddyji a little table covered with a white cloth, on which are set out a Gillette safety razor, a badger shaving brush, a dish of soap, a hand mirror, and a plastic jug of hot water. Bill adds to these a couple of bottles of Imperial after-shave lotion that he has spied in an open cupboard. The lotion was a present, and Daddyji hardly ever uses it. Bill drags first Daddyji in his chair and then the table into the light by the back window, where Ivan is setting up the camera. The light falls in such a way that on film it will seem as if Daddyji were in a palatial room.

"Won't this very fancy shot exaggerate Daddyji's social station?" I ask Bill.

"Of course," he says. "Contrast between your father and Chacha is just what we want."

The shooting begins with Chachaji sitting on the bed and watching Daddyji lather his face.

Daddyji, his voice muffled by the towel bunched up under his chin, asks Chachaji how he is getting along in his job at the chemical-supply shop.

Chachaji answers in a vague, polite way. This morning routine has been enacted between Chachaji and my father for something like half a century. Chachaji, usually laconic in his requests (probably so that he can back away with dignity at the first sign of resistance), suddenly turns talkative and delivers himself of one of his longest speeches in English—first asking for an old razor blade, and then, when he is given one, thanking Daddyji effusively. He seems to be learning how to please Bill, and, indeed, Bill is delighted with his speech.

Daddyji also hams it up a bit for the camera, giving Chachaji a second razor blade, which is new, and warning him not to cut himself with it. Chachaji's whiskers are so soft and his razor blades so dull, as a rule, that the new blade could indeed be a hazard.

"You are very kind to me," Chachaji says. "You have shown great sympathetic consideration toward me. I am very thankful to you that you have given to me two blades."

"Well done, Chacha—you spoke like a true gentleman!" Bill cries when the shooting stops.

"Cran Sahib is a true gentleman himself," Chachaji says.

We have Chachaji at our disposal for the rest of the day, and I suggest to Bill that we do a shot of him walking along an ordinary street as a contrast to his walking in the bazaar.

"Great," Bill says. "Let's do a tracking shot on a road somewhere, with the sky in the background. It will suggest a puny, insignificant man against the universe."

We drive to Mathura Road, the main road in the neighborhood—which, since it is Sunday, is almost deserted—and Ivan takes tracking shots from the station wagon as Chachaji walks along. Bill and I follow Chachaji at a discreet distance on foot.

Suddenly, Chachaji stops.

"Continue, continue, Chacha!" Bill cries.

But Chachaji won't budge. "I see her. There, at the window, Chopra Sahib's one and only wife. If Chopra Sahib comes to know that I am photographing myself in front of his house, he will certainly dismiss me."

We immediately stop filming and drive Chachaji back to his house.

Bill says that he has been struck by the way Chachaji slowly and carefully bolts and locks his door. "It's symbolic of how Chacha guards what little he has. I want the bolting and locking on film." After Calcutta, Bill is taking an interest in Chachaji's minutest actions.

"The next thing you'll want me to shoot is Chacha paring his fingernails," Ivan says as he takes the shot.

"I want to do more with the pink turban, too," Bill says to me. "How does he wash it? How does he starch it? How does he tie it? I may be able to include that whole routine in his waking-up scene."

When I ask Chachaji, he says that he does all these things himself. Washing and starching the turban, however, take several hours, so Bill settles for a shot of him just tying the turban.

Tying a turban is a swift and intricate task, and it is a good half hour before we get a decent take.

"I wonder if Bill is cracking under the strain," Eoin says to me. "This locking-doors and tying-turbans business is pure petit-point stuff. It's the kind of embroidery that producers go in for when they run out of ideas."

"If I'd had my way, I would have had Bill doing sequences like this all the time," I say to Eoin. "The humdrum minutiae of the day—those are what keep Chachaji going."

March 13th

THIS AFTERNOON, BILL ABRUPTLY SAYS, "I HATE talking-head situations, but let's give the idea you had a whirl—let's film some of your clan sitting around and just talking about Chacha."

"But that will give the impression that they sit around and gossip, and may reflect badly on them," I say. "What I would like would be interviews with one or two people at a time."

"We don't have time for individual interviews. But

if the general talk comes out looking bad, we won't use it."

We all arrive unannounced at Mahesh's and Nimi's. Umi, who is going to a party later on, is here, too, dressed in her best sari and wearing a lot of jewelry. Nimi, on the other hand, is dressed casually, in what would look to a Westerner like a sleeping suit. Nimi's teen-age daughter Gita and Umi's teen-age daughter Indira are also here. I tell my sisters and nieces about Bill's idea. Umi feels she should be dressed more simply, but Bill likes the contrast between her style of dress and Nimi's. As it happens, Umi's elegance and Nimi's nonchalance in dress are characteristic.

Bill picks out the most luxuriant spot in the garden of the government residence, and seats the two mothers and two daughters around a garden table. He hands them some empty teacups and saucers. Eoin says that the cups will sound empty, and asks for some tea, but Indira, who is drinking Coca-Cola, quickly puts some in everyone's cup. Bill tells the women to say anything about Chachaji that comes into their heads, and the camera and tape recorder are turned on.

The women talk in a seemingly uninhibited way. Umi sees the humor in Chachaji, Nimi the pathos. Indira is soulful about him, Gita scornful. If the two sisters set each other off, so do the mothers and daughters. The conversation flows easily along and is dramatically effective, but I feel that there is something artificial about it. Ordinarily, I am sure, they would never say, or think, the things they now find themselves saying. They talk about Chachaji's being cuckolded. Their conversation sounds affectionate but also patronizing, until one remembers how much they all do for Chachaji, and that they are talking mostly about events that happened forty years ago. And, irrespective of what they say, the setting is too lush, the contrast between the life of my sisters and nieces and that of Chachaji too painfully evident, the moment too intimate, for me to feel comfortable about the sequence.

"They look marvellous," Bill says, in his most upbeat manner. "They are a marvellous double act. The pathos and the humor are exactly what the life of Chacha is about. If their English sounds intelligible once we get back to Boston, I can certainly see using them in the film as a sort of a Greek chorus." Then, in a typical switch, he adds, "But things that look good at the time of shooting often don't look good in the editing room. This scene may fall flat on its face when we start working on it."

Mamaji drops by and says that she has just received word that Chachaji's wife, Tara, died while we were in Calcutta.

"Damn!" Bill says to me under his breath. "I wish we could have filmed her cremation. It would have made a marvellous sequence."

"I wonder if we can use the Tara scene in the film now," I say. "I certainly don't think we can use the sisters and nieces talking about her."

"Why not?"

"On grounds of taste," I say. "Her death casts the scenes in a very different light."

"I disagree," he says. "Who will ever know? And anyway her death only makes our little scene more dramatic."

March 14th

W HEN WE COME DOWN IN THE MORNING FOR BREAKfast, there is a telex for Bill from Chris Gilbert, the production manager in Boston. It is the first written response to the rushes we've had, and it reads:

HAVE VIEWED ROLLS 3-8. NO DISASTERS. HOWEVER, SEQUENCE OF UNCLE WALKING INTO WORK PLACE (PHARMACY OF PROSPERITY) IS SLIGHTLY OVEREXPOSED—SOFT FOCUS—DEPTH OF FIELD VERY SHALLOW FOR DAYLIGHT. ALL SUBSEQUENT ROLLS DAYLIGHT FOCUS/LIGHT LEVEL FINE.

LATHE BRACELET MAKER CLOSE-UPS NOT CLEARLY SHOT FROM SIDE. CAN BE CUT, BUT NOT WELL UNDERSTOOD. NEED OVERSHOULDER OR HIGH SHOT TO LOOK WELL. BUS FOOTAGE WILL BE A HUMOROUS HIGHLIGHT.

BOTH DAVID [FANNING] & I FEEL THAT UNCLE IS EMERGING AS A STRONG FIGURE. HE MAY HOLD WHOLE FILM. RESERVE JUDGMENT TILL YOU SEE.

WE HAVE AN APARTMENT FOR YOU WHEN YOU RETURN TO BOSTON. KEEP US INFORMED ON YOUR RETURN PLANS.

IF YOU IDENTIFY THE SOUND REEL, WE WILL BEGIN TRANSCRIBING IN ADVANCE.

CIAO, CHRIS

"I wish they had told me twenty sleepless nights ago that Chacha looks strong enough to hold the whole film," Bill says.

As a joke, Bill hands the telex to Chachaji, who is breakfasting with us.

Chachaji reads through it slowly, uncomprehendingly, and then hands it back. "Cran Sahib uses a lot of capitals," he says.

Between periods of driving Chachaji around to do Chopra's errands with dispatch, we spend the day filming Chachaji with his replacement, Chachaji at a ration shop, Chachaji with his son, Chachaji with his grandson—all little more than cameos but, with Bill's newfound enthusiasm for the film, all important for filling out the Chacha story.

"Come to think of it," Bill says, "we'd better just do a few shots more—of Chacha at the railway station, to complete the train sequence to the village. Then we'll be through."

So that's how we spend the afternoon.

We are scheduled to leave for home early on the morning of the eighteenth, and Bill has decided that we should all spend the next two days on a sort of busman's holiday, visiting the Taj Mahal and the nearby Moghul city of Fatehpur Sikri, to do some sightseeing.

Ivan, Ved, and Sally at Fatehpur Sikri

March 17th

S HOOTING IS OVER, AND WE LEAVE LATE TONIGHT: Bill for Boston, to edit the film, after a couple of days' stopover in London to see his parents and to choose some archival footage for flashbacks; Araminta, after a stopover in Dubai, for Toronto and her job; Ivan, Eoin, and Jane for their separate homes in London, to wait for word of their next assignments; Sally for New York, to look for a new job; and I also for New York, to resume my writing life.

We spend the day shopping and packing, and in the evening I give a dinner for everyone—my parents, my sisters, their husbands and children, Chachaji, and the team—at the India International Center, the headquarters of an association for Indians and foreigners here. Chachaji, however, mysteriously fails to show up.

"The lights at his house were off, so we thought he was already here," Mamaji says. "He must have forgotten."

I send Yoginder Singh to look for him.

Ivan, Eoin, and Jane stand in a corner, suddenly shy of mixing with my family, as if they were already mentally adjusting themselves to leaving.

"I wish we'd got old Chacha a present," Ivan says. "He worked awfully hard and got so little out of it."

"Such presents are traditionally the responsibility of the producer," Eoin says.

"Still, it would have been nice to get something for him from the crew," Jane says.

I tell them not to worry—that Mamaji will give Chachaji a present from them—and I draw them into conversation with Daddyji.

Bill comes over. "I've already settled up with Yoginder Singh and Amarjit Singh," he says. "I tipped them each two hundred rupees—I was running a bit short. They saluted, but went away grumbling. What did they expect?"

"Well, that tip might have done from an Indian," I say. "But they probably expected five times that from you. I will tell Mamaji to give them a little something extra."

The dinner is predictably bittersweet. There is a certain amount of forced gaiety. What makes us especially sad is that Chachaji never comes; we may not have a chance to thank him and say our goodbyes.

After dinner, the members of the team hastily take leave of my family, and we go back to our hotel to catch a little catnap before our flight, which is due to depart at 2:30 A.M.

March 18th

A T ABOUT MIDNIGHT, THERE IS A KNOCK AT MY door. It is Yoginder Singh, who has finally found Chachaji at a relative's house and brought him to the hotel. As Mamaji thought, he had completely forgotten about the dinner.

"He's waiting downstairs in the coffee shop," Yoginder Singh says.

I telephone the news to Bill and go downstairs.

Practically the first thing Chachaji says to me is that he is hungry. I order him a supper of tea, toast, and an omelette.

One by one, everybody in the team comes down, looking a little sleepy. No one seems to know what to say to Chachaji, except for Bill, who asks him questions about his day and laughs even louder than usual at Chachaji's funny-sounding English answers. The others laugh nervously and sporadically.

Chachaji busies himself with buttering his toast and pleasurably slurping his tea.

Bill suddenly stands up and makes a little speech. "Chacha, it has been a great privilege and an honor to know you," he says. "You have given us all the facilities for photographs."

Everybody laughs, but Chachaji is concentrating on his omelette and doesn't seem to take in the fact that Bill is addressing him.

I translate, and Chachaji says, "Cran Sahib has all the facilities for a gentleman."

Bill now presents Chachaji with a squarish cardboard box. Chachaji struggles to open it, but he can't. Bill takes it from him and yanks it open. Inside is a small, Indian-made transistor radio. At first, Chachaji looks disappointed; if he was going to get a present at all, he would no doubt have preferred money. But then he smiles in delight; he likes to go to my parents' house and listen to the news on the radio, and now he has a set of his own.

Chachaji and Bill both try to get the radio to work, but its batteries are apparently dead. Finally, Yoginder Singh plugs it into an electrical outlet, and the tinny sound of a film star singing a love song fills the coffee shop.

"Good brother," Chachaji says to Yoginder Singh, "Cran Sahib has made me remember my lusty youth."

March 26th

L ATE IN THE EVENING, BILL CALLS ME IN NEW York from Boston. (Our arrangement is that he is to screen the rushes and edit and assemble the major sequences; then I am to fly up to Boston regularly to work with him.) He is out of sorts. Except that WGBH has found him a nice apartment, everything seems to have gone wrong.

"I tell you, on my first day here I should have been able to walk into a cutting room at nine o'clock

At the Taj Mahal
Left to right: Eoin, Sally, Ved, Jane, Araminta, Bill, and Ivan

in the morning and find all the rushes developed, edge-numbered, and synched up," he says. Edge numbers are put on the film for editing purposes, and "synched up" refers to the synchronization of sound and picture. "I should have been able to cut the first sequence if I wanted to. But I've been here five bloody days, and so far, out of the sixty-four exposed rolls of film, the GBH people have only got the first twenty-four rolls ready." Bill, who took pride in his economical use of film stock, had exposed only sixty-four rolls out of the WGBH allowance of a hundred and eight. "I have, of course, screened all twenty-four," he continues. "They say they won't have the rest of the rolls ready until late next week. What was the point of going through the trouble and expense of shipping all the film from India? The GBH people will cost me nearly two weeks of valuable editing time, just out of bone idleness. I tell you, there's a casualness about this station, a nine-to-five union mentality among members of the staff. The moment it's five, they all run home, and some idiot security man comes and locks my office—if you can believe it—so I can't even get at my notes and stills. I'm damn irritated. I'm damn mad."

Knowing that Bill has a tendency to exaggerate his frustration when things don't go precisely his way, I sympathize with him and then ask him what he thinks of the twenty-four rolls of film he has seen.

Suddenly sounding cheerful, he launches into a lengthy commentary on the rushes, jumping from sequence to sequence. "We've got several nice shots of Chacha looking very lugubrious at the luscious sing-song. The contrast is terrific. The shot of old Chacha

arriving at work at the chemist's is not out of focus, as
alleged by GBH in the telex to us in India. In fact,
there is a nice slight bonus in that our two takes of
that look different enough so that we can use one take
for his arriving at work and another for his going back
to work after a 'mission.' If we can make anything at
all of your niece's wedding, it will have to be pretty
impressionistic. But, luckily, we've got two shots of
Chacha at the wedding: one in which he's tossing
flower petals at the bride, and one in which he's sitting
on the ground singing to himself—though, unfortu-
nately, we don't have a lot of his song. He stopped
singing just as we started filming. The shots of his
early-morning routine look and sound really beautiful;
the expression on Chacha's face is lovely—it's very determined and intense. There's one disappointment with
the visit to his son and daughter-in-law—Chacha talks
very little. This is a bloody nuisance. In so many shots,
we see him shuffling around, blundering around, not
talking to anyone, that I was hoping that in this sequence we would hear the sound of his voice, which
has such a distinctive flavor to it. Dinner with your
family is great. Everything essential—all the great
shots of Chachaji—are on the first roll, and this is
lucky, because the GBH people were right about the
second roll of the dinner being scratched. The second
roll does have one rather nice shot, taken from the
kitchen door, of the whole family sitting around the
table. But the shot is wide, so maybe we can cut around
the scratch. The color and the lighting of the bed-tea
sequence are marvellous, even if no one notices such
things on American television. One piece of good news

is that the sound is of exceptionally high quality throughout. It's really very classy, authentic sound. When Chacha is shaving, you can hear the rasp of the razor blade on his tough old skin louder and clearer than you could hear it even when we were shooting. Again and again, subtle effects come out sensationally. In a feature film, you would record the sound effects in perfect studio conditions and splice them into the sound track for maximum effect. Eoin gets these sounds in the most imperfect conditions and they're just terrific."

March 29th

A NOTHER LATE-EVENING CALL FROM BOSTON. BY now, Bill says, he has all the rolls of film in hand and has screened all the rushes.

"Sometimes things look better on the screen than they did when you were involved in shooting them on location," he says. "The bit where your father intervenes on behalf of Chacha and talks to the president of the wretched sect is nothing visually, but it's very powerful. Though your father talks in a funny sort of mixture of Hindi and English and it's hard to follow him—still, as the scene goes on, you gather that Chacha's very home and livelihood are threatened. Again, when we were shooting the sequence of Chacha at his house with the young yogi, it just seemed pretty ordinary, but on the screen it's terrific. The sequence says that here is Chacha, living in this ridiculous house *cum* temple where weird religious cranks go to worship, and he's standing around, as old as can be, watching this strongly improbable-looking young man contort himself into silly shapes. Of course, no documentary cameraman whose work I know can touch the sheer beauty of Ivan's photography. But this has its drawbacks. The village just looks too pretty. After you have looked at the first four or five pretty shots, they start to cancel each other out—another picturesque bullock cart in a picturesque field makes you want to throw up. But then again Chacha riding up to the village in the trap is one of my favorite shots in all the rushes."

"Why is that?"

"Both the horse and Chacha look as if they were arrested at some earlier point in evolution." He laughs. "There are many other bonuses in the village. When we were filming the hay-cutting sequence, it was quite windy. At the time, you couldn't really hear the wind, but you could see the men's clothes kind of flapping around them. By some acoustical freak, the microphone caught the sound of the wind, and you hear it all through the sequence. This sound gives the village a rather bleak and lonely feeling. It emphasizes the hopeless situation of the villagers. As for Calcutta, the cremation sequence turned out to be really disappointing. The shot of the mourners lifting the corpse onto the pyre is very good, but Ivan, in his zeal to get it on film, did not control it—there is too much smoke against the gray sky. But then it might not have worked anyway. The cremation sequence is a perfect example of things looking worse on the screen than they did on location, when you were emotionally involved with them. But I'm beginning to sound negative, so let me tell you about the gem of all the sequences. It's the one in which Chacha is scrounging razor blades off your father. One thing that is nice about it is that you can understand his English—hearing it, I really laughed out loud. Another thing that's nice is that he really looks pathetic and comic at the same time. One of the secretaries here walked in and saw him glowing with his blades, and said, 'He looks awfully sweet. Who is he—Ved's father?' I tried to explain the Mehta genealogy to her, without success."

I ask Bill when he hopes to have all the major sequences edited and assembled.

"I don't know yet. For logistical reasons to do with cutting rooms and editing machines, I cannot make my magical first cut until next Monday. That'll already be April 3rd."

Fanning had told us that he hoped to broadcast the film on June 15th, and I ask Bill if he now thinks we can have the film ready by then.

"I can have the film ready to go in May, but the GBH people are talking about putting off our broadcast until the thirteenth of July. What has happened, in effect, is that, through some quirk in planning, the three original GBH productions for 'World'—about race in Britain, about life in Bogotá, and ours—are going to be completed around the same time. So they will have to be bunched up in the last three slots of the viewing season—the fifteenth of June, the twenty-ninth of June, the thirteenth of July. Since audiences fall off precipitously in July, I am lobbying for the mid-June slot for us. I'm going around saying hello to station mucky-mucks to see if I can't get our film put ahead of the others."

April 3rd

"T his was my happiest day," Bill says over the telephone late in the evening. "I've made my magical first cut. I wangled the best cutting room in the studio, with a good, clean editing machine, which has two picture tracks and two sound tracks, so that the editor and I can work at the same time."

"Who is your editor?"

"Oh, haven't I mentioned him yet? He is called Eric Neudel. We viewed all the rushes together. Now we'll be working on the more difficult sequences together; that is to say, strings of pictures that have to be made into sequences: the Delhi railway station, Chacha getting on the train, and so on—times when we had to hassle to get pictures and couldn't really develop sequences on the spot. The assistant editor, Mark Erder, is working on a smaller editing machine, assembling the natural sequences, like Chacha's early-morning routine, which goes together like butter and mashed potatoes."

"What do Eric Neudel and Mark Erder make of Chachaji?"

"I don't know about Mark—he's an uncommunicative sort—but Eric just cackles away and rubs his hands when he sees Chacha shuffling along. Eric thinks Chacha is charismatic, which isn't quite the word I would use. He said to me, 'It's going to be a real pleasure to spend the next several months looking at Chacha.' We were lucky in our crew. Well, we've hit it lucky again in our editor."

It is strange to think of two new people in Boston involved with Chachaji—even if it is only on film—and I ask Bill what, exactly, their role is.

"Theoretically, I could tell Eric or Mark that I want this shot, this shot, this shot, in sequence, and to cut it in just that way, but I would no more think of doing that than I would think of telling Ivan exactly how he should take a shot, because the editor, like the cameraman, has his own creative contribution to make. When Eric and I are viewing the takes together, I mention the bits I like in a take and what I want to get out of a sequence. He talks back and tells me the bits he likes. We toss it around, and then I give him his head. Then, when I see what he's done, how he's cut a scene, we may talk some more and he may have to recut it. It's a collaboration all the way."

April 6th

A NOTHER LATE-EVENING CALL FROM BILL, WHO IS eager to discuss with me some ideas about the structure of the film.

"What do you think of starting the film with some sort of montage of peak moments in Chacha's day?" he asks. "My instinct would be to build the montage around a tracking shot of him walking along the road, which would have the flavor of the beginning of an Italian neo-realist film. And we would just walk him, walk him, walk him—all the time showing this curious old man, with the film title up over it. The trick would be to show the long tracking shot and quickly slap on it a series of dissolves and superimpositions of those peak moments—Chacha waking up, Chacha getting washed, Chacha taking the bus—so that you would always be aware of Chacha walking in the background. We could put funny old English music to it, and you could say in your commentary, 'Keep up to the end of the road.' We could close the film with another montage, this time of peak moments in Chacha's life journey—Chacha in the Ganges, maybe the cremation ground in Calcutta—built on the same long tracking shot of Chacha walking along the road, so that the effect of the ending would be the equivalent of a long zoom back."

"But if you start with this montage business, it'll be very confusing," I say. "We'll have to do a lot of explaining about who Chachaji is and what he is doing, which will mean heavy commentary at the top of the film. The commentary would be off-putting—would take away from the power of the pictures."

"How would you begin it, then?" Bill wants to know.

"I would perhaps begin with a sort of night-dawn opening—his house at night, dawn breaking over the house, Chachaji waking up, putting on his turban, doing his ablutions. Such an opening would be simple and natural, and would require only minimal commentary—actually, just a phrase or two, stating, 'This is my poor relation, this is the house where he's lived for twenty years.'"

"The morning stuff is really terrific, but I hate to send in my best cavalry at the beginning of the battle. Besides, although the pictures are great, the dawn makes for a very slow opening. A viewer will be five minutes into the film without knowing or caring what's happening—he will just be watching some old man wake up and get washed. I want a slam-bang opening."

"On the contrary, I think the night-dawn opening would make you curious," I say. "You'd want to know who this old man is and what he's getting ready for. Anyway, the opening should grow out of the material of the film, not be imposed on it."

"I'll talk it over with Eric. By the way, I've obtained some very nice archival footage in London for flashbacks, and I've had it processed so that it can be used with our stock. I was thinking that on one side of the frame you could show Chacha in his house, drinking his tea—as it happens, he's drinking it greedily and noisily—and on the other side you could show archival footage of British pomp and power, of famine and plague. You could lay your commentary over the split frame, and say that Chacha is drinking tea, and that he grew up under the British raj and his mother died in a plague epidemic. The split frame is almost in bad taste, but I think it will strike a pathetic-comic note."

"Bill, no split frames. Keep it simple."

We both laugh.

April 15th

B ILL AND I HAVE NOT MET SINCE INDIA, AND NOW that he has edited and assembled the major sequences, I have come to Boston. I go to Soldiers Field Road—to the Allston area—where WGBH has some of its studios, in two low, characterless buildings within about a hundred yards of each other. I go to the building in which Bill has his cutting room, follow a claustrophobic narrow, meandering corridor past windowless cubicles and small, functional rooms, and arrive at Bill's door. Just inside the door, in a sort of antechamber, sits the assistant film editor, Mark Erder, winding and rewinding spools of film and tape. All around him are racks filled with flat cardboard boxes and small, round tins, all bearing labels like "Chacha Leaves House/Turban," "Yogi Man," "Razor," "New Man/Chacha's Successor," "Ablutions," "Tea Shop/Walk (Sky)," "Flashback Trims," "Chacha's Wife," "Hardwar—Dip."

Bill's own room is so small and crowded that there

Jane and Ivan

is scarcely space enough for two people to sit. One end is almost entirely taken up by a big editing machine, and all around are bins and racks overflowing with more labelled boxes and tins. Here and there, strips of film hang from hooks and racks like spaghetti.

"Oh, hello," Bill says, scarcely looking up from the editing machine and without taking his pipe from his mouth. He pulls up a stool for me, and goes on, "You've missed Fanning. He sort of drifted in yesterday for about ten or fifteen minutes and watched a couple of sequences. He was all dressed up in a suit and said, 'I'm going to Washington.' And I said, 'Are you going there to ask for money?' He sort of chuckled, so I'm sure that was it." He laughs, and goes back to his machine.

Bill and Eric Neudel—a friendly, thin, dark, intense man, smoking a cigarette—are in the middle of looking at the family-dinner sequence. They turn on the machine, and there is Chachaji at the dinner table, almost dwarfed by it and by the towering members of the family all around him. Everyone is talking, laughing, and eating, and Chachaji is reciting an Urdu quatrain. I feel homesick.

"What is he saying?" Bill asks, stopping the machine.

I translate:

> There was a mud lamp burning at my tomb.
> He came, lit his cigarette,
> Used the oil to massage his head,
> And departed.

"Did he really say that?" Eric says, his eyes widening. "It's so moving."

"I wish to hell he'd been moving in English," Bill says. "Maybe you can give the gist in your commentary." He puffs on his pipe and reaches for a tin marked "Sisters."

I ask him about the system of labelling.

"We've cut up the footage into major sequences and shots, and labelled them," he tells me. "Whenever we need to find a sequence or a shot, instead of screening an entire roll we can usually just reach for it on one of these racks. Say you have a shot. You've been looking at it for a week of editing. You've always been a little unhappy with it. You suddenly realize that the shot is a tiny bit too short. If it were extended a tenth of a second, it would become a perfect shot. Unless you have properly marked and labelled all the strips of film, you can spend hours looking through hundreds of feet of film for just a few frames. We could be looking for a tenth of a second, or four-fifths of an inch, of film in the almost twelve hours, or twenty-five thousand six hundred feet, of film we shot in India."

Bill threads the "Sisters" sequence onto the machine and turns the machine on. By some trick of the camera, the garden in which my sisters and nieces sit looks even more lush than it did at the time of shooting. Moreover, their conversation has been edited—reordered and pointed up—so that, for instance, their remarks about Chachaji's having been cuckolded sound not affectionate, as they did at the time, but harsh and a little cruel.

I wonder aloud whether my sisters and nieces don't come off sounding unsympathetic and unfeeling.

"I think their comic-tragic view of Chacha is very true to life," Bill says. "A man can slip and fall and break his nose and you might feel sorry for him but it would still be funny. Chacha is just one of those unfortunate beings with a funny broken nose."

"But I don't think laughing at someone's being cuckolded is in good taste," I persist.

"But didn't they joke about it? Didn't they laugh about it?" Bill asks.

"But in editing you've pointed it up," I say. "Besides, we set them in front of the camera and told them to talk about Chachaji. If Eoin, Ivan, Jane, and Sally were put in front of a camera and asked to talk about you, they might find themselves saying all kinds of things that ordinarily they would never say—things that would be out of character."

"Hell, I just don't see what's out of character," Bill says. "I just don't see it the way you see it. Your reaction may be colored by the fact that you are a member of the family."

"But what do you think Chachaji and Madan would feel if they saw the scene? Isn't that worth worrying about?"

"Who cares?" Bill says. "Who knows whether they'll ever see it or understand it? Besides, what does Chacha know about film? What do you think, Eric?"

"I have to say I agree with you, Bill," Eric says. "In fact, they are such powerful women that they steal the show."

"But that's the last thing I want them to do," I say.

"What do you think, Mark?" Bill calls out.

"About what?" Mark calls back.

"About the sisters and the nieces."

"I don't know."

"I'll see what Fanning thinks," Bill says. "But I think they're great."

May 5th

A NOTHER IN A SERIES OF VISITS TO ALLSTON. Together, Bill, Eric, and I screen the working rough cut, which, though it is much longer than the designated length of fifty-seven minutes and has many uneven spots, is quite miraculous. Once again, Bill has astonished me. During the shooting, I often wondered whether Bill understood what Chachaji was about. During earlier sessions in Allston, I wondered about Bill's judgment and taste. But the rough cut has a meditative tone, a certain lyrical calm. It consummately conveys Chachaji's spirit, and most of it is in good taste. It's as though Bill's frenetic pyrotechnics on location and his brashness in the initial editing were just a camouflage for his innate poetic sense, for his instinctive understanding of Chachaji and, by analogy, of India.

"Well, what do you think?" Bill asks.

"It's very moving," I say. "The film has a certain stillness, which is just right."

"Can you be specific about what you like?" he asks.

"One thing I like is that in many stretches the shots seem to be held for a longer time than they usually are in documentaries, so that details really emerge. I especially like the slow night-dawn opening."

"What else?" Bill asks.

I refer to our old dispute about material extraneous to Chacha's story. "I'm relieved that you decided to leave out the Calcutta stuff."

"I tried and tried, but what can I tell you?" Bill says. "In the end, those sequences just couldn't be made to fit into Chacha's story."

"There are many other things in the film I like—"

Bill interrupts. "What bothers you? You must have criticisms."

"I am still troubled by the sisters and the nieces," I say.

"That's probably just you," Fanning says, joining us. "I agree with Bill and Eric. The women look and sound terrific. We'll just have to agree to disagree on that."

"You can put a line or two in your commentary saying how much your sisters and nieces help Chacha and take care of him," Bill says good-naturedly. "Anything else you don't like?"

"The ending is really abrupt," I say. "The Hardwar scene is over before it gets started. I always imagined that it would be one of the most lyrical passages in the film."

"When Eric and I got down to cutting it, everything besides Chacha's dip seemed distracting," Bill says.

"But we don't get a sense of place or occasion," I say.

"I am of the same opinion," Fanning says. "I think the Hardwar scene should be two or three times its present length."

Bill and Eric look thoughtful.

"What about lengthening the scene by using the singing of the blind musician as a motif, and intercutting shots of him singing with general shots of the bathers in the river—all building up to Chachaji's own ritual bath?" I say.

Everyone more or less agrees to give the idea a try, and then Fanning leaves.

May 18th

B ILL COMES TO NEW YORK TO FILM ME FOR THE prologue. (Neither of us particularly wanted a prologue. We thought that the film should speak for itself. But Fanning felt that the night-dawn opening Bill and I finally settled on— Chachaji's house at night, Chachaji waking up, tying his turban, doing his ablutions—was too slow for American viewers, and that the film needed a sort of teaser to establish me, Chachaji, and the theme of India.) Bill has brought along a tall, muscular black cameraman, Dasal Banks, from the WGBH staff. (Ivan was unavailable—he was off in some corner of the Mediterranean.) Bill does a tracking shot of me walking along Fifth Avenue near my office, on Forty-third

Street, and then rushes off with Banks to film the view of Manhattan from Brooklyn Heights.

That evening, he calls me and suddenly sounds very excited about the prologue. "We can make it a real attention-getter," he says, "showing you living in New York, thinking about Chacha in India."

I have learned by working with Bill in Allston that his editing is as controlled and careful as his talk is flamboyant and loose, so I simply reply, "As Chachaji would say, 'I know you will treat it like a gentleman.'"

May 26th

A GAIN IN ALLSTON, THIS TIME WITH THE FINAL script of my commentary, which I have been working on for the past three weeks, sometimes reading it against the new, final rough cut to get the words to coincide with the pictures. In the new cut, the scene with my sisters and nieces is no better, but the revised Hardwar ending is marvellous.

I go into a soundproof booth, which is furnished with a chair, a microphone, and an intercom for communication with Bill, who sits outside at a control panel with Steve Izzi, the sound mixer. Bill is equipped with a stopwatch, a copy of my commentary, and a list of the shots to which the commentary is keyed.

"O.K.? Are you relaxed?" Bill calls to me through the intercom. "Do you have plenty of water? Just try to strike that slightly amused tone that we generally used in talking about the old sod in India. Let's take you through the prologue. Cue One. Recording."

I take a deep breath and say into the microphone, "For the last thirty years, I have lived in the United States and Great Britain, and I am now an American citizen—"

Bill interrupts. "Put a little smile in your voice. You sound a little lugubrious. Again, Cue One."

"For the last thirty years, I have lived in the United States and Great Britain, and I am now an American citizen—"

Bill interrupts again. "You're reading too slow. You're going over by almost four seconds. You'll cover all the New York traffic sounds. Again, Cue One."

I say in rapid fire, "For the last thirty years, I have lived in the United States and Great Britain, and I am now an American citizen."

"Now it sounds like 'Jabberwocky.' Can you rewrite and shorten the line?"

Bill waits while I cut and recast the sentence.

"Again, Cue One."

"For the last thirty years, I have lived in the West, mostly in New York."

"Over the top—that's fine. Cue Two."

"I live in Manhattan, an island of immigrants within a nation of immigrants. My name is Ved Mehta."

"Forget it," Bill interrupts. "We'll be over the shot of the Taj Mahal by the time you get to your name."

I drop the "immigrants" sentence. I am learning

that the discipline of television writing is a bit like that of writing haiku, but with little poetry.

"Cut Cue One and Cue Two together."

"For the last thirty years, I have lived in the West, mostly in New York. My name is Ved Mehta."

May 30th

B ILL BRINGS A VIDEOCASSETTE OF THE ROUGH CUT down to New York, and we take it over to the offices of the Public Broadcasting Service, at Rockefeller Center, where we have arranged to meet the Indian Public Relations Consul, A. G. Thakur, who has been designated by the Indian government to make an appraisal of the film. He is the first Indian-government official to view the film, and our commitment to the Indian government is that we will try to meet any "objection" that Thakur makes, and will not broadcast the film without a "no objection" letter from him.

Thakur arrives with a colleague from Washington, and they both watch the film without expression. The film is, of course, still in a working version; the commentary and natural sounds overlap, and sometimes the commentary runs over and explains a picture that has already gone by. Still, by and large it gives a fairly accurate impression of what the finished film will be like. Though Bill laughs raucously at every funny passage—as if he were seeing the film for the first time—the two officials don't so much as smile, and they depart without a comment.

"God, what do you suppose that means?" Bill asks. "That they don't like it?"

"Not at all," I say. "They probably want to compare notes before committing themselves. In the Indian government, no one likes to take responsibility for anything unless he can share it with someone else."

"Even if they don't like it, we're going to broadcast it," Bill says. "We'll make our stand on freedom of the press. Anyhow, there's hardly any time left to diddle with the film." Bill has managed to get the broadcast of our film scheduled for the fifteenth of June—ahead of the two other WGBH original "World" productions.

"Let's not cross that bridge until we come to it," I say.

"But I wish they had said something," he says.

As soon as I reach my office, I get a call from Thakur. "I say the film was beautiful," he says. "There is nothing objectionable in it, except for the vultures eating the carcass of a holy cow." Thakur is a devout Hindu. "I'm not saying those things are not seen in India, but . . . " He trails off.

I start explaining to him Bill's reasons for including the vulture shots in the storm sequence, but he cuts me off. "Please do not bother," he says. "I will send you a 'no objection' letter tomorrow. If I may add a personal note, the film is very true to Indian life."

June 13th

BILL CALLS FROM BOSTON. HE HAS FINISHED DOING everything—mixing the final version of my commentary and the sound in with the pictures, getting the film and the opticals (archival flashbacks and special effects) printed, screening the test print, getting the colors adjusted, screening the final print—but instead of sounding elated he sounds low. "In spite of all the care we took with timings and all the cuts we made the last time we recorded your commentary, the commentary was still too long," he says. "When we came to mix it, it didn't always hit the right picture, or crowded out things like the wonderful flapping sound of old Chacha putting down the prayer rug. In mixing, I had to be ruthless with the commentary. You may not agree with my cuts, but what can I say? There was no time to consult you. We were right down to the wire."

Changing the subject, I ask him what he thinks of the final print.

"What can I tell you? The station really let me down badly. Before I went to India, I told the GBH people that I would probably want to do some elaborate opticals, and that they should book us time in a good optical house. Cutting opticals is a special skill, because they're all made up of special effects, and a film cutter in an ordinary laboratory simply can't handle them. The station failed to do what I had asked. Luckily, our flashbacks turned out to be simpler than I had originally imagined, or we would have had a real mess on our hands. Still, I'm not happy about the grading of colors on the opticals. The GBH people also failed to book time with a good laboratory for cutting the negative, so we ended up using some undistinguished place that made a lot of mistakes."

"What kind of mistakes?"

"Well, we had marked the film so that after the prologue we would start with a very simple title, white on black—'Chachaji, My Poor Relation: A Memoir by Ved Mehta'—and then fade up to a first shot of Chacha's house at night. Instead of a fadeup, they made a cut from the title to the house. I had a long fadeout at the end of the Hardwar sequence, and they made it into a short fadeout—instead of slowly easing out the scene, they hacked it. Worst of all, for some reason the laboratory got some sort of particles all over the negative, which show up on the print. The particles are so fine that no one but a cameraman or a producer would notice them, but they detract at least one per cent from my pleasure in seeing the film."

"But aside from your vexation over all the technical defects, what do you feel about the film as a whole?"

"Normally, when I finish a film I never think about it—it's just a number on a list of films—because until the making of 'Chachaji' I'd been mostly stuck with stock journalistic stuff. But with 'Chachaji' I just keep thinking about it, actually dreaming about the bloody thing. I keep thinking that somehow we might have made it better. Working on this film has been one of the most amazing creative experiences of my life. It has opened the mental doors to a whole new world for me."

June 15th

T HIS IS THE DAY OF THE FILM'S BROADCAST. BILL has flown home to Toronto to watch the broadcast with Araminta, and I have Sally and a few other friends over to my apartment to watch it with me. Although I have been involved with the film at every stage, the realization that it is now going to appear to the American and Canadian public, at a designated time, on a regular channel, gives me the odd sensation that I am coming to it as a stranger.

I am surprised all over again at how true the film is to Chachaji's spirit—a remarkable accomplishment, since so many people who helped to shape it had at most a cursory acquaintance with Chachaji. Even the prologue, despite its disparate, clashing elements (New York and India, the Taj Mahal and Calcutta), somehow succeeds in striking the right note.

The first section of the film, constructed around a typical day in Chachaji's life in the city, shows Chachaji in an ironic, amusing light. A mouselike figure in a bright-pink turban, he is seen being shoved aside, laughed at, ignored, and patronized. We see him as an old, poor, eccentric, proud, solitary man, defending himself against the bullying world by sticking to little rituals and routines. We learn that he lives like a poor relation and works as a clerk, and that his needs are as elemental as those of his poorer brethren—centering mainly on eating. We discover through flashbacks and through the conversation of his relations that he has been bedevilled by calamities; for instance, he can't even be certain which of the four children he thought he had fathered are his. Despite his travails, he is consistently portrayed as having a certain amount of natural elegance and dignity.

The second section of the film, constructed around a journey, shows Chachaji in a warm, affectionate light. We see him travelling to the village, and, by extension, to village India, where he was born and brought up. We gather, through a flashback, that he lost his home, his ancestral village—almost his world—during the religious wars over the creation of Pakistan in 1947. We see him moving about the bleak, backward, crumbling village where some of his poorer relations have settled, and we perceive village life as at once changeless and precarious—nature as at once life-sustaining and destructive. Chachaji seems oddly out of place in the village—an effect that makes us realize that although in city surroundings he appeared innocent and insignificant, in village surroundings he is sophisticated and important.

If the first two sections of the film are essentially descriptive, the third, and last, section has the texture of a short story. Constructed around a time when everything begins to go wrong for Chachaji, it shows him in a pathetic, almost tragic light. After Chachaji leaves the village, a vicious hailstorm nearly lays it waste. When he gets back to the city, a similarly vicious household storm nearly lays waste the pattern of his life. In his absence, a much younger and more vigorous man has been hired to perform many of the duties that Chachaji has been performing to earn his room and board. Chachaji manages to survive this latest crisis, but we are left in no doubt that he is infirm and all but defeated as he struggles to keep his balance in the vortex of Indian poverty. We follow him on his day's rounds and see how the people he especially honors and reveres (government functionaries and the like) spurn and reject him. Even shopkeepers, who are lower in station than he is, heap insults on him. Yet he is stoical and dogged in his endurance, perhaps because his struggle is not without purpose. Much as he is supported by his better-off relations, so, in turn, he supports a little family of relations poorer than he is—the family of the one son who acknowledges him as his father. (It is as if the whole society were held together by a chain of relatives, one only slightly less poor and dependent than the last.) Then we see him in a sort of "Last Supper" scene with his little family, on the eve of a sort of penitential journey to the sacred Ganges. There we see him communing with the river and taking the traditional Hindu cleansing bath for salvation. The last image we have is of Chachaji, turbanless and—except for a towel around his middle—naked, shivering on the steps of the Ganges.

The film works well when the focus is on Chachaji and his struggle to survive, perhaps because, in a sense, it is a reflection of the struggles of hundreds of millions of his countrymen, who, of course, have their own individual stories to tell. It exploits brilliantly the special gifts of the visual medium—conveying in a few shots, for instance, the horrors of taking a bus in India, which would require pages of description in a book. The film works less well when it tries to describe social complexities—the difference between the social standing of Chachaji and that of his better-off relations—perhaps because of the device it uses: a single conversation of four women (my sisters and nieces) is cut into segments, and the segments are dropped into the film at strategic moments, with the women made to serve as a sort of Greek chorus. We are never sure from the snippets of conversation whether the women are well intentioned or malicious, whether Chachaji deserves their criticism or is an innocent victim of their sarcasm. (They even joke about Chachaji's being cuckolded.) Their character is all the more puzzling because we are told that they have always helped to take care of him, even though he is only a cousin twice or three times removed. (In the West, someone like Chachaji would very likely be committed to an old people's home by his own children.) Moreover, the contrast between the women's situation and Chachaji's is so blatant (they sit in a very rich-looking garden drinking tea, while he seems to have no place to rest and can scarcely afford tea) that the device borders on cinematic rhetoric, and intrudes on the lyrical mood of the film.

The chorus of women, however, is a minor, if irritating, distraction in a film that is simple and touching over all, for we never really lose sight of Chachaji or the meaning of his story. The film has a certain unfolding intensity. (As Bill had hoped all along, the film received a prize: a duPont-Columbia Award for Excellence in Broadcast Journalism for 1977-78.)

Epilogue

A FTER THE TURMOIL OF THE BROADCAST (SALLY, Sally's mother, and Sally's sister felt sad because Bill listed everyone but her in the credits), I write a longish letter to Chachaji, enclosing many newspaper and magazine stories about him which feature his picture. Around the same time, Bill posts the following letter to Chachaji, with a copy to me:

Canadian   Société
  Broadcasting   Radio-
    Corporation   Canada
                                                    June 20th, 1978
DEAR BAHALI RAM,
    Here are the snaps I promised to send you. Your picture has appeared in many newspapers in America. Many people saw the film and were very interested in what they saw. Most people liked the pictures in the village (especially the Swami) and the scenes at Hardwar best.
    I would like to thank you for all the help you gave us when we were in India. I hope I come back again soon and meet you again. We all send you our warmest greetings and say "thank you for your great sympathetic consideration."

                                                    Yours sincerely,
                                                    William Cran

A few weeks later, I receive this letter from Chachaji:

NEW DELHI
July 8, 1978

DEAR MR. VED MEHTA,

We have not heard from you since your departure. I hope you are enjoying good health.

Here all are keeping good health. You will be glad to know that William Cran sent us some photographs. Please convey him my thanks. You have not sent us any photograph. You know that my wife passed away two days before you left here. Please do send us some photographs of my wife and my family by the return of post. Please write about your health also. My son Madan is anxious about the photographs of my wife Tara as she is no more on the earth. Please do sent me some photographs as early as possible.

I have heard that my picture is going on the New York Television and my picture was published in many newspapers. Please do write me more about my picture. I hope you will pay us a tour early in future. Please bring me an electronic watch as my old watch is gone out of order. I shall be eagerly waiting for your visit.

Remember me to Baily [Sally] and rest of your company.

Once again I would like to remind you to send me photographs.

Your well wisher
BAHALI RAM
D-24 Nizamuddin East
N. Delhi
India

At first, I am a little taken aback by the stiff, formal, and also importunate tone of Chachaji's letter, but then—as I hasten to send him some stills of his wife and some duplicates of the newspaper and magazine clippings about the film, since it seems my first batch went astray—I reflect that the letter is in English, and was written by a poor man to a relation who, for all its writer knows, lives like a king in a fairyland.

As it happens, Chachaji did see the film—I was able to show him a videocassette of it during a visit to India. He watched it, stunned and riveted, sitting on the edge of his chair with his hands between his knees— clutching the chair as if he were afraid that he might fall off. The only time he said anything was when his wife appeared on the screen. "Even that!" he exclaimed. At the end, I asked him if he liked the film. "Like it?" he said. "If I do not like it, who will like it? Wonderful! Was that really me? Was it a dream? It seemed as if I was having a holy audience with myself in Heaven."